More
Paper, Paint, and Stuff

Karen B. Kurtz

with photographs by Mark A. Kurtz

Scott, Foresman and Company
Glenview, Illinois   London

Good Year Books
are available for preschool through grade 12 and for every basic curriculum subject plus many enrichment areas. For more Good Year Books, contact your local bookseller or educational dealer. For a complete catalog with information about other Good Year Books, please write:

Good Year Books
Department GYB
1900 East Lake Avenue
Glenview, Illinois 60025

*To Clifford and Eleanor Swartzendruber
and Ezra and Grace Kurtz
who have all helped
to make us part of who we are*

Contents

LET'S GLUE

LET'S PAINT

LET'S WEAVE

LET'S GIVE GIFTS

LET'S GO INTO THE PAST

LET'S READ AND APPRECIATE

LET'S THINK

LET'S TRAVEL

Preface and Acknowledgments

Here is a source book of art activities for you and your child that helps you combine fun, learning, and quality time.

Although intended primarily for teachers to use in their classrooms, kindergarten through third grade, **More Paper, Paint, and Stuff** tries to meet the creative art needs of others as well. Parents and grandparents can also discover the joy of doing art projects with young children. Camp counselors, scout leaders, Sunday school teachers, and day care supervisors are certain to find these activities a welcome addition to their programs.

Every activity in this book has been used successfully in pre-schools and elementary schools for more than ten years. Many have been published in national children's magazines. All feature clear step-by-step directions and require only easily obtainable, inexpensive materials. In addition, most relate well to major subject areas of the elementary curriculum: science, language arts, social sciences, mathematics, and social development.

More Paper, Paint, and Stuff encourages children to tap their inherent creativity. All of the chapters present projects that emphasize active learning—"making and doing." These projects help develop an awareness of others by cultivating new thoughts, experiences, and problem-solving techniques. Other creative helps include the variations that follow many of the projects, photographs, drawings, patterns, hints, and recipes.

Be creative—let all these elements suggest new possibilities to you. Let each activity motivate you to try new experiences and to customize projects to fit your situation. Children can inspire you with their creativity and zest for life; this book can serve as a bridge between generations seeking to share the joy of creating together.

More Paper, Paint, and Stuff came about as a result of the enthusiastic reception given our first book: **Paper, Paint, and Stuff** (Scott, Foresman and Company, 1984). We would like to thank Lois Bare, Lois Kurowski, Myrna Kaufman, Ann Graber Miller, and John D. Yoder at Goshen College in Indiana for their encouragement. And we would like to express our appreciation to special friends Rose Widmer and Lois Myers who have always believed in us.

—KAREN AND MARK KURTZ

Introduction

Children need to become excited and enthusiastic about the wonderful world in which they live. They must also learn how to think creatively and critically, appreciate others' points of view, and develop a positive self-concept. It is in the classroom that this unique blend of intellectual, social, and emotional development takes place.

The primary focus of **More Paper, Paint, and Stuff** is on active learning that enhances this development. Active learning brings the child's whole self to bear on the situation at hand, providing enough security for him or her to interpret the world and his or her experiences in it. Offering scores of creative art ideas, this book emphasizes "making and doing" with ideas for gift giving, working with others, and relating to everyday experiences. Children participate in high-level positive learning experiences through cutting paper, observing themselves in a mirror, writing stories, and other forms of active involvement.

By exploring new experiences, thoughts, and ideas, children become more empathetic, more knowledgeable, more appreciative, more understanding, and more aesthetically attuned to life. They move from asking "What has happened in the past in my world?" to "What will happen in the future in my world?" Through experiences in problem-solving, children can enhance their development of positive social values.

Using the Activities, Patterns, Drawings, and Photographs

Clear step-by-step directions accompany each activity. If any adult preparation needs to be done in advance (such as collecting, arranging, or preparing items), that preparation is specified. Most of the activities also include variations that explain additional ways to follow up or alter the learning experiences.

The photos, drawings, and patterns display the results you can expect to see. All patterns are full size. You need not use the patterns, however, in order to do the activities successfully. In fact, you need not know much about art at all to enjoy doing the activities in this book. Be creative! Adapt the activities for your own use.

Working with Groups of Children

You can often save time and effort by having children work on activities in small groups. Some of the projects work very well when done cooperatively by groups of three or more children. Pay attention to the items listed under the heading "The Group Needs"; these are items that the group can share during the creative process.

Try grouping tables together and letting the children stand around the area. Spread newspapers in one area to contain such messy activities as painting, using wet chalk techniques, assembling a mural, gluing a sculpture, or cooking.

Encourage freedom of discussion. Remember that it takes time for young children to develop their independence; encourage it to blossom and grow.

Finally, be sure to consult the "More Helpful Hints" section at the back of the book for a variety of time-saving techniques, ranging from tips on collecting items for the activities to ideas for displaying the projects when they are completed.

Nuts and Bolts Mobile

Each Child Needs:

a dowel rod or stick, about 8 to 12 inches long

three or five assorted lengths of yarn

about 20 inches of string for hanging

glue

The Group Needs:

assorted nuts and bolts

Procedure:

1. Attach nuts and bolts to each piece of yarn.

2. Attach the pieces of yarn to the stick. Be sure to vary the lengths of yarn.

3. Tie the hanging string around each end of the stick.

4. Balance the mobile and hang.

Variation:

Visit a company that uses nuts and bolts in its business or a person who uses nuts and bolts in his or her job. Write a story about the visit.

Me

Each Child Needs:

a piece of paper as large as the child

scissors

The Group Needs:

marking pen

assorted tempera paints

brushes

newspapers for covering work area

Procedure:

1. Each child lies down on the paper, posing in an interesting manner. Hands and feet may show body movement.

2. Using the marking pen, draw around the child to make a life-sized outline.

3. After the child gets up off the paper, cut around the outline.

4. Use the tempera paints to create clothing on the paper. Add features and accents.

5. Let the paper dry.

6. Be sure the child's name appears on the paper. Display each posed outline as a sculpture. Seat the pieces of paper in chairs or attach them to walls.

Variations:

1. Use crayons instead of tempera paints for the clothing and features.

2. If the children are responsible enough to do this activity independently, divide the class into pairs or into groups of three or four. Let them draw around each other and paint each other's imaginary clothing.

3. Hold up one completed sculpture and talk about the real person. Encourage the children to say something they like about that person. Repeat this procedure for all the sculptures.

4. Have the children bring in an object that has special meaning to them, like a baby snapshot or a hat. Place the object so that the sculpture seems to be holding it and fasten both the sculpture and the object to the wall.

From *More Paper, Paint, and Stuff*, published by Scott, Foresman and Company. Copyright © 1989 Karen B. Kurtz and Mark A. Kurtz.

Green Tree Mobile

Each Child Needs:

one 12x18-inch sheet of green
construction paper

about 18 inches of yarn

a shorter string for hanging

glue

scissors

The Group Needs:

paper punch

construction paper scraps

glitter

Procedure:

1. Fold the construction paper in half, matching the long edges. Crease.

2. Cut the folded paper diagonally from the outer lower point to the opposite corner. When unfolded, the paper will form a triangle. This makes a tree shape.

3. Refold the paper. Cut the tree into three sections by making two horizontal cuts.

4. Lay down the three sections, keeping them in order from top to bottom.

5. Punch holes at the outer edges of each section.

6. Connect the sections by tying yarn through the holes. Leave about two or three inches of yarn between the knots and trim off any excess yarn at each end. Be sure to keep the tree sections parallel.

7. Decorate the tree by gluing on assorted scraps of construction paper or glitter.

8. Attach the string for hanging.

From More Paper, Paint, and Stuff. published by Scott, Foresman and Company, Copyright © 1989 Karen B. Kurtz and Mark A. Kurtz.

Chick Peas and Toothpicks

Advance Adult Preparation:

Soften a package of dried chick peas by soaking them in water overnight. Collect several boxes of round toothpicks.

Each Child Needs:

an assortment of softened chick peas

several round toothpicks

one 4-inch square of cardboard for base

glue

Procedure:

1. Talk about the idea of sculpture as building upward from a strong foundation. Relate the idea to building a house with four or more walls resting on a foundation and a roof overhead.

2. Place three chick peas in a triangle on the table. Connect them with toothpicks by gently pressing each chick pea on the end of a toothpick. The chick peas will hold securely when they dry out.

3. Create a sculpture by building up, over, out, and around. Add more peas and toothpicks as needed. The sculpture is complete when it looks pleasing to the child.

4. Glue the sculpture to the cardboard base and display.

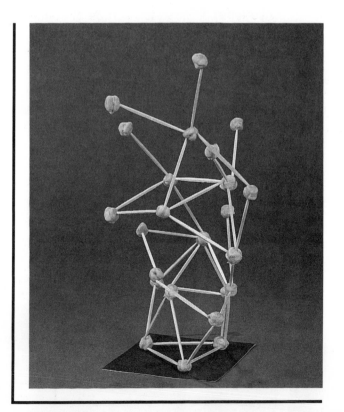

From *More Paper, Paint, and Stuff*, published by Scott, Foresman and Company, Copyright © 1989 Karen B. Kurtz and Mark A. Kurtz.

Wall Hanging

Advance Adult Preparation:

Go for a walk and collect lightweight, forked tree branches. If necessary, cut a larger branch down to size.

Each Child Needs:

one forked branch, about 12 inches long

scissors

assorted pieces of yarn

Procedure:

1. Attach yarn to the branch by weaving it over and across open spaces, looping it around the branch, or dangling it down from the branch. The design is finished when it looks pleasing to the child.

2. Trim excess yarn from the ends.

3. Display on a wall or on a table.

Red-Tongued Monster

Advance Adult Preparation:

Use oaktag to prepare the pattern on page 115. Prepare the puppet by folding one 12x15-inch sheet of construction paper in half, matching the short edges. Fold in half again, matching the long edges. Unfold the second fold so that the paper now measures 7½x12. Slip your fingers between the top and bottom of the paper and fold up the corners marked A and B. Then flip the paper over and fold up the corners marked C and D on the other side. Fold up corners E and F. Slip your fingers between the top and bottom of the paper again and refold on the second crease, folding corners C and D to E and F. Flip the paper over and repeat with A and B.

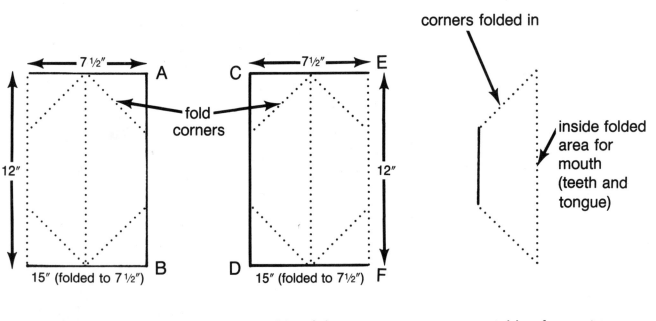

one side of the paper   other side of the paper   outside of monster

Each Child Needs:

one puppet (prepared as above)

one piece of red construction paper large enough for the tongue

construction paper scraps

scissors

glue

The Group Needs:

patterns for the monster's eyes, teeth, and tongue

From *More Paper, Paint, and Stuff*, published by Scott, Foresman and Company. Copyright © 1989 Karen B. Kurtz and Mark A. Kurtz.

Procedure:

1. Use the patterns to cut out the parts of the eyes. Assemble and glue to the monster.

2. Use the patterns to cut out the teeth and tongue. Glue inside the monster's mouth.

3. To make the monster move, hold it in your hand and fold or cup it in half.

Variations:

1. Use the monster to dramatize stories and poems.

2. Use the monster with shy or withdrawn children or with those having special needs.

3. Share monsters with another group of children.

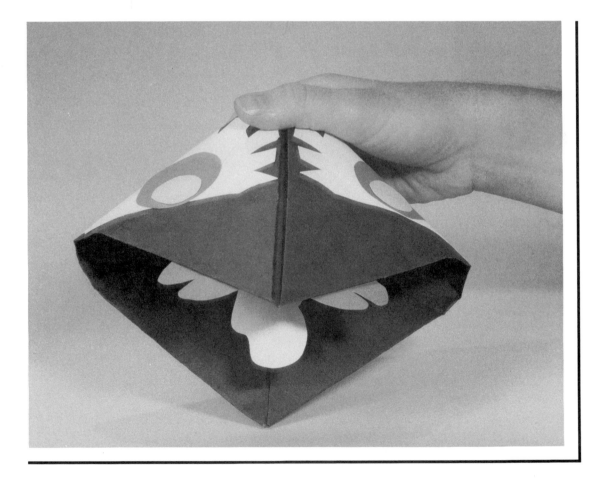

Wood Scrap Sculpture

Advance Adult Preparation:

Collect wood scraps of various shapes and sizes. Contact a carpenter or lumber yard for these supplies.

Each Child Needs:

11 or 13 assorted wood scraps for the sculpture

glue

one gummed label

Procedure:

1. Talk about sculpture. Discuss shape, size, and balance.

2. Arrange the wood scraps into an interesting design, using all of them. Although the children may need a good deal of time to develop a pleasing design, you may find it helpful to set a time limit for arranging.

3. When the child is satisfied with the design, glue the wood scraps together.

4. Write the artist's name and the title of the sculpture on the label and attach it to the sculpture.

From *More Paper, Paint, and Stuff,* published by Scott, Foresman and Company. Copyright © 1989 Karen B. Kurtz and Mark A. Kurtz.

House

Advance Adult Preparation:

Collect used Christmas cards, large ones (at least 6x8 inches). Use oaktag to prepare the patterns on page 116.

Each Child Needs:

five Christmas cards

patterns, as above

pencil

scissors

masking tape

Procedure:

1. Using the fronts from four Christmas cards, draw around the end and side patterns of the house. Cut out two from each pattern.

2. Tape together on the inside like a box. Stand up on the table to make a dimensional house.

3. Open and place the last (uncut) card on the top of the house to make the roof. Tape in place.

Variations:

1. Display several houses together in a row or in groups.

2. Fold additional Christmas cards back in half, matching the long edges. Cut diagonally to create Christmas tree shapes. Decorate the trees with glitter and cluster them around the houses.

From More Paper, Paint, and Stuff, published by Scott, Foresman and Company. Copyright © 1989 Karen B. Kurtz and Mark A. Kurtz.

Stone Stew

Advance Adult Preparation:

Read *Stone Soup* by Marcia Brown (Scribner) and discuss together.

Each Child Needs:

small bowl or large mug   napkin

plastic spoon

The Group Needs:

4 pounds stew meat, chunked

½ cup flour

2 tablespoons oil

2 quarts water

6 medium potatoes, diced

2 turnips, diced

3 carrots, diced

3 ribs celery, diced

2 green peppers, diced

1 onion, diced

2 tablespoons salt

4 beef bouillon cubes

3 round smooth stones, cleaned

hot plate

large stock pot or pan for making stew

assorted measuring utensils

knife

large wooden spoon

potholders

crackers

Procedure:

1. Roll the pieces of meat in the flour.

2. Brown the meat in hot oil and cover with water.

3. Simmer for two hours, adding more water as needed.

4. Add vegetables, seasonings, and stones. Cook about 30 minutes or until vegetables are tender.

5. Dish up stew in bowls, serve with crackers, and enjoy! This recipe makes 16 to 20 servings.

Variations:

1. While the stew is simmering, make a batch of cornbread. Serve the cornbread with the stew, along with glasses of milk.

2. Share the stew with another group.

3. Have the children copy while you dictate either the directions for or a story about making stone stew.

4. Have the children tell another group how to make the stew.

From More Paper, Paint, and Stuff, published by Scott, Foresman and Company. Copyright © 1989 Karen B. Kurtz and Mark A. Kurtz.

Peanut Butter Play Dough

Each Child Needs:

a piece of waxed paper

newspapers for covering work area

The Group Needs:

6 cups powdered milk

3 cups honey

6 cups peanut butter

large bowl for mixing

spoon

blunt knives or cookie cutters or
rolling pins for shaping

Procedure:

1. Blend all the ingredients together—first with the spoon and then with your hands.

2. When the ingredients are thoroughly mixed, separate the dough into balls and place on waxed paper sheets. Give one ball of play dough to each child. This recipe makes enough dough for 15 to 20 children.

3. Shape the dough into snakes, peas, cookies, and pizzas.

4. Cut the dough with blunt knives or cookie cutters, or roll it with a rolling pin.

5. When finished playing with the dough, eat and enjoy!

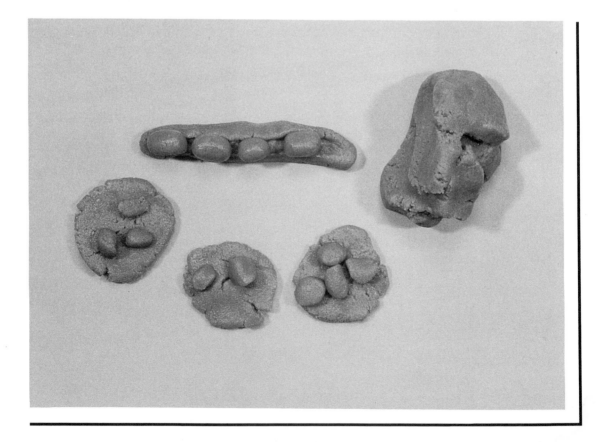

Party Mix

The Group Needs:

1 box round oat cereal

1 box square rice cereal

1 box stick pretzels

1 pound peanuts

garlic salt, to taste

2 sticks margarine, melted

2 teaspoons Worcestershire sauce

hot plate

large bowl

saucepan

oven

2 cookie sheets

plastic sandwich bags for storage

Procedure:

1. Mix the cereals, pretzels, and nuts together in the large bowl. Sprinkle the mixture with garlic salt.

2. Use the hot plate to melt the margarine, and then add the Worcestershire sauce. Pour this mixture over the ingredients in the bowl and mix well.

3. Spread the ingredients on the cookie sheets. Bake at 250 degrees for about one hour.

4. When the mix is cool, package in sandwich bags. This recipe makes a snack for 15 to 20 children. Enjoy!

From *More Paper, Paint, and Stuff*, published by Scott, Foresman and Company. Copyright © 1989 Karen B. Kurtz and Mark A. Kurtz.

Bird Feeding Tree

Advance Adult Preparation:

Purchase suet meat at the supermarket meat department.

Each Child Needs:

two lengths of yarn, one about 24 inches for stringing and the other about 8 inches for the cup handle

The Group Needs:

suet, in chunks

stale doughnuts

popcorn

round pretzels

cranberries

ice cream cones

large-eyed tapestry needles

living evergreen tree or discarded Christmas tree

Procedure:

1. Thread the longer length of yarn into the tapestry needle.

2. String together assorted pieces of suet, doughnuts, popcorn, pretzels, and cranberries on the yarn.

3. Remove the needle and knot each end of the yarn.

4. Tie several of these food-laden strings together.

5. Fill the cones with suet chunks and popcorn. Attach yarn handles to the cones to make cups.

6. Place the strings and cups on the branches of the tree. Watch the birds enjoy the feast!

Variations:

1. Decorate a pair of trees.

2. Make one bird feeder tree for each window in the room.

Pinecone Bird Feeder

Each Child Needs:

two large pinecones

about 18 inches of yarn

a piece of waxed paper, large
enough to cover the pinecones

scissors

The Group Needs:

5 cups of cornmeal

5 cups of peanut butter

2 cups of raisins, chopped nuts,
or sunflower seeds

large bowl

several knives

newspapers for covering work
area

Procedure:

1. Attach the yarn securely around each pinecone.

2. Mix the peanut butter and cornmeal together in the bowl.

3. Add the other ingredients and mix again.

4. Use the knives to spread the mixture on the pinecones. Be sure to fill the indentations in the pinecones liberally with the mixture.

5. Wrap each pinecone in waxed paper for transporting home.

6. Hang the feeder by laying the yarn across a tree branch.

From *More Paper, Paint, and Stuff*, published by Scott, Foresman and Company. Copyright © 1989 Karen B. Kurtz and Mark A. Kurtz.

Tea Bag People

Each Child Needs:

one tea bag (flow-through type)

one Styrofoam cup

one plastic stir stick

scissors

The Group Needs:

bowl

teapot filled with boiling water

tea strainer

sugar

lemon slices

small brushes

tempera paints—flesh-colored, red, blue, green, and orange

rickrack, glitter, and construction paper scraps

newspapers for covering work area

Procedure:

1. Remove the tea bag from its packet.

2. Spread the tea bag apart and cut along its bottom fold line. Cut off and discard its hang tag.

3. Collect all of the loose tea, put it in the bowl, and save for making hot tea.

4. Gently open the tea bag. The top portion will become the person's face and hat; the bottom portion will become the person's body and clothing.

5. Cut out the hat shape from the top half of the bag.

6. Use the flesh-colored tempera paint to paint the face. Use the other colors to paint the hat and clothing. Allow the paint to dry.

7. Steep hot tea in the teapot and strain before serving in cups. You may want to add sugar and/or lemon slices.

8. After the paint dries, decorate the hat with glitter and the clothing with rickrack. Create facial details (like eyes and mouth) from the paper scraps and glue in position.

From *More Paper, Paint, and Stuff*, published by Scott, Foresman and Company, Copyright © 1989 Karen B. Kurtz and Mark A. Kurtz.

Making Butter

The Group Needs:

1 pint whipping cream

glass jar with a tight lid

salt, to taste

plate or butter mold

spatula

large bowl

Procedure:

1. Pour the whipping cream into the jar.

2. Seal the jar tightly.

3. Have the children take turns shaking the jar until the whipping cream separates into buttermilk and butter. While the children are doing this, talk together about living independently as the pioneers did as opposed to living more interdependently as we do today.

4. Place the butter in the bowl and add salt.

5. Use the spatula to press against the butter in order to remove excess buttermilk.

6. Pat the butter into a butter mold or form it on a plate.

Variations:

1. Drink the buttermilk or bake with it.

2. Spread the butter on crackers or bread and have a tasting party.

3. Draw sequential pictures about the butter-making process.

4. Have the children describe the process for making butter while an adult writes down the recipe. Duplicate the recipe and distribute it to the children so that they can take the recipe home with them.

From *More Paper, Paint, and Stuff*, published by Scott, Foresman and Company. Copyright © 1989 Karen B. Kurtz and Mark A. Kurtz.

Reindeer Sandwiches

The Group Needs:

2 pounds ham salad

2 to 4 loaves brown bread

1 package stick pretzels

1 bottle maraschino cherries

1 bottle ripe olives, pitted

spreaders or knives

plates or trays

Procedure:

1. Trim the crusts from the bread.

2. Make ham salad sandwiches.

3. Cut each sandwich into two triangles.

4. Make each triangle into a reindeer by adding a half cherry for the nose, two olive slices for the eyes, and four pretzel sticks (stuck into the ham salad) for the antlers. Enjoy!

Variation:

Serve reindeer sandwiches at a Christmas party with milk and ant logs (decorated celery sticks filled with peanut butter and topped with raisins).

Boo!

Advance Adult Preparation:

Use oaktag to prepare several copies of the pattern on page 117.

Each Child Needs:

one 9x9-inch sheet of
   construction paper

a dowel stick, about 12 inches
   long

scissors

pencil

glue

The Group Needs:

transparent tape

several patterns, prepared as above

Procedure:

1. Fold the construction paper in half.

2. Lay the pattern over the paper, matching the fold lines, and draw around it.

3. Carefully cut out the mask.

4. Glue and tape the mask to the dowel stick.

5. Using the dowel as a handle, place the mask over your eyes. Boo!

From *More Paper, Paint, and Stuff*, published by Scott, Foresman and Company. Copyright © 1989 Karen B. Kurtz and Mark A. Kurtz.

Indian Mask

Advance Adult Preparation:

Use oaktag to prepare several copies of the pattern on page 118. Purchase feathers at a crafts store.

Each Child Needs:

one 9x12-inch sheet of brown
   construction paper

two 18-inch lengths of yarn

scissors

crayons

glue

The Group Needs:

several patterns, prepared as above

feathers

stapler

Procedure:

1. Fold the construction paper in half.

2. Lay the pattern on the paper, matching the pattern to the fold line, and draw around it with a brown crayon.

3. Carefully cut out the mask.

4. Unfold the paper. Use black crayon to add a line across the forehead for the Indian's headband and to create circles around the eyes.

5. Use crayons to decorate the mask, pressing heavily on the paper.

6. Glue several feathers above the headband.

7. Staple one length of yarn to each side of the mask for tie strings.

8. Put the mask over your face, and tie the strings at the back of your head.

Turkey Mask

Advance Adult Preparation:

Use oaktag to prepare several copies of the pattern on page 119.

Each Child Needs:

one 6x9-inch sheet of brown construction paper for turkey head

one 4x6-inch sheet of yellow construction paper for beak

one 2x6-inch sheet of red construction paper for wattle

crayons

glue

scissors

two 18-inch lengths of yarn

The Group Needs:

several patterns, prepared as above

stapler

Procedure:

1. Fold the brown paper in half.

2. Lay the pattern on the paper, matching it to the fold line, and draw around it with brown crayon.

3. Carefully cut out the mask.

4. Unfold the paper. Use black crayon to outline and enlarge the eyes.

5. Fold the yellow paper in half, matching the long edges. With the fold in hand, cut off the ends of the paper diagonally to make the beak.

6. Glue the beak to the mask.

7. With a wavy motion of the scissors, cut off one end of the red paper to make the wattle.

8. Glue the wattle underneath the beak.

9. Complete the turkey head with crayons, pressing them heavily onto the paper.

10. Staple one length of yarn to each side of the mask for tie strings.

11. Put the mask on your face, and tie the strings behind your head.

From *More Paper, Paint, and Stuff*, published by Scott, Foresman and Company, Copyright © 1989 Karen B. Kurtz and Mark A. Kurtz.

Birthday Crown

Advance Adult Preparation:

Use oaktag to prepare the pattern on page 120. Cut out the crown from two 8x18-inch sheets of oaktag, sizing the crown to fit the birthday child's head. Use a marking pen to write the name of the child on the front of the crown.

Each Child Needs:

one crown, prepared as above

The Group Needs:

crayons

construction paper scraps

glitter

tempera paints in small containers

brushes

fabric

mesh produce bags for the veil

egg carton sections

glue

scissors

newspapers for covering work area

Procedure:

1. The group decorates the crown as desired, gluing an assortment of items in place.

2. Give the crown to the birthday child.

Three-Cornered Hat

Advance Adult Preparation:

Use oaktag to prepare several copies of the pattern on page 121.

Each Child Needs:

one pattern, prepared as above

three 4½x12-inch sheets of blue construction paper for the hat

one 4x12-inch strip of red construction paper for the feather

scissors

crayons

pencil

The Group Needs:

stapler

construction paper scraps

Procedure:

1. Lay the pattern on the blue construction paper and cut it out. Repeat for all the sheets of paper.

2. Staple the corners together, sizing the hat to fit the head.

3. Fringe the long edges of the red construction paper strip to make the feather. Curl the fringed strip over a pencil, press, and release.

4. Glue the feather inside the hat.

5. Use crayons or glue cut-outs from construction paper scraps to add accents.

6. Wear and enjoy!

From *More Paper, Paint, and Stuff*, published by Scott, Foresman and Company, Copyright © 1989 Karen B. Kurtz and Mark A. Kurtz.

Fancy Hat

Each Child Needs:

one grocery bag for the hat

1x12-inch strips of assorted construction paper for the hair

scissors

glue

crayons

The Group Needs:

mesh produce bags for the veil

pipe cleaners for the flower stems or antennae

construction paper scraps for the flowers

Procedure:

1. Fold the grocery bag flat.

2. Cut all around the bag about six inches from the bottom. It is the bottom part of the bag that will make the hat.

3. Decorate the hat by gluing curled construction paper strips for the hair, a mesh bag for the veil, and pipe cleaners for antennae or flower stems.

4. Use crayons to add accents.

5. Wear and enjoy!

Variations:

1. Hold a spring bonnet parade.

2. Share your creations with other groups.

3. Use the fancy hats as accessories when acting out plays, stories, or poems.

From *More Paper, Paint, and Stuff,* published by Scott, Foresman and Company. Copyright © 1989 Karen B. Kurtz and Mark A. Kurtz.

African Mask

Advance Adult Preparation:

Collect one-gallon plastic milk containers.

Each Child Needs:

one milk container, as above

yarn

glue

scissors

The Group Needs:

an assortment of items for decorating the mask: wooden spools, beads, telephone wire, seashells, feathers, small coins with holes, buttons, soft drink tabs, cardboard cones, paper curls, rickrack, glitter, old jewelry, chains, small mirrors

white tempera paint in small containers

dark tempera paints in small containers

brushes

paper punch

marker pen

newspapers for covering work area

Procedure:

1. Use the marker pen to draw the shape of the mask on the inverted container. The handle becomes the nose.

2. Outline and cut out the eyes.

3. Cut off the rest of the milk container from the mask area.

4. Paint the mask a dark color and let it dry.

5. Use the white paint to add geometric shapes or straight lines around the nose and eye areas. Let dry.

6. Use the paper punch to punch holes through the mask's forehead, around the outside, and under the eyes. Tie yarn through some of the holes for fringe or hair.

7. Decorate the mask with various items, fastening each one with the telephone wire, threading it on the yarn, or gluing it in place.

8. Wear the mask or hang it on the wall.

From *More Paper, Paint, and Stuff,* published by Scott, Foresman and Company, Copyright © 1989 Karen B. Kurtz and Mark A. Kurtz.

Wig

Each Child Needs:

two 4x18-inch strips of purple construction paper for the headband of the wig

two 3x18-inch strips of purple construction paper for the crown of the wig

glue

The Group Needs:

1x6-inch strips of assorted construction paper for the hair

Procedure:

1. Wrap the 4x18-inch strip of construction paper around the head, measuring to fit.

2. Cut the strip to size and glue the ends together. This makes the headband of the wig.

3. Glue the two 3x18-inch strips inside the headband, at right angles to each other. This makes the crown.

4. Loop and curl the 1x6-inch strips of construction paper to create the hair.

5. Glue the hair to the headband and crown. The wig is finished when the hair looks full and balanced.

6. Wear and enjoy!

Variation:

Use any extra construction paper strips to create a curled paper beard or mustache. Fasten to the skin with transparent tape and use along with the wig to complete the costume.

From *More Paper, Paint, and Stuff*, published by Scott, Foresman and Company. Copyright © 1989 Karen B. Kurtz and Mark A. Kurtz.

Calendar

Advance Adult Preparation:

Collect old calendars, each one at least 9x12 inches.

Each Child Needs:

one calendar, as above

crayons or pencil

Procedure:

For beginning practice in writing, copy a number or letter in each block on the calendar.

Party Place Markers

Advance Adult Preparation:

Collect white plastic hosiery eggs.

Each Child Needs:

one half of a white plastic hosiery egg, as above

felt tip markers

Procedure:

1. Using a black or dark-colored marker, print your name on the front of the egg.

2. Use other colors to decorate the egg with designs.

3. Display the place markers and use them as decorations at your next party!

Variation:

The children can make place markers for each other instead of for themselves.

From *More Paper, Paint, and Stuff*, published by Scott, Foresman and Company. Copyright © 1989 Karen B. Kurtz and Mark A. Kurtz.

Myself

Advance Adult Preparation:

Display one or several large mirrors (preferably as big as the children) in the room.

Each Child Needs:

one 12x18-inch sheet of drawing paper

scissors

crayons

Procedure:

1. Discuss with the group how people are alike and different.

2. Let the children observe themselves in the mirror, individually or in small groups. Encourage each child to note distinctive characteristics; listen to his or her responses.

3. Have the children use crayons to draw their self-portraits.

4. Have the children use scissors to cut out their self-portraits.

Variations:

1. Instead of cutting out the portraits, use them as book covers.

2. A child may tell his or her own autobiography to an adult who writes it down, or the child may write down the story him- or herself. Display the stories and portraits together.

3. Compile the self-portraits into a book, and place it near other books for reading or browsing. You might also let the children take the book home overnight to share with their families.

Open Windows

Advance Adult Preparation:

Use oaktag to prepare several copies of the patterns on page 122.

Each Child Needs:

one 9x12-inch sheet of colored construction paper for the house

one 9x12-inch sheet of contrasting colored construction paper for the background

one 6x9-inch sheet of red construction paper for the roof

crayons

scissors

The Group Needs:

several patterns, as above

Procedure:

1. Lay the house patterns on the construction paper, draw around the patterns with crayon, and cut out the house.

2. Lay the roof pattern on the contrasting construction paper, draw around it, and cut out the roof.

3. Fold back the windows as indicated on the house patterns.

4. Glue the house to the background.

5. Glue the roof in place.

6. Use crayons to draw pictures in the windows of objects that begin with sound-symbols. For example, an eight or acorn begins with the "a" sound; snake, Sally, or soup begins with the "s" sound.

7. Complete the picture with crayon accents such as grass, a path to the house, people, flowers, or clouds.

From *More Paper, Paint, and Stuff.* published by Scott, Foresman and Company. Copyright © 1989 Karen B. Kurtz and Mark A. Kurtz.

Dancing Snowman

Advance Adult Preparation:

Collect new, unused tongue depressors or ice cream sticks. Use oaktag to prepare several copies of the pattern on page 123 and cut them out.

Each Child Needs:

one 3x6-inch sheet of white construction paper for the snowman

crayons

glue

scissors

The Group Needs:

several patterns, as above

construction paper scraps for the scarf and top hat

Procedure:

1. Place the pattern on the construction paper, draw around it, and cut out the snowman.

2. Cut out the scarf and top hat from the construction paper scraps and glue to the front of the snowman.

3. Use crayons to add accents such as eyes, nose, smiling mouth, and buttons on coat.

4. Glue the tongue depressor or ice cream stick to the back of the snowman.

5. Place the end of the stick in your mouth and wiggle your tongue up and down to make the snowman dance.

From *More Paper, Paint, and Stuff*, published by Scott, Foresman and Company, Copyright © 1989 Karen B. Kurtz and Mark A. Kurtz.

Designs

Advance Adult Preparation:

Collect lids from cottage cheese, yogurt, sour cream, or baby food containers.

Each Child Needs:

one lid, as above

one 9x12-inch sheet of drawing paper

crayons

Procedure:

1. Lay the lid on the drawing paper to use as a pattern.

2. Use a black or other dark-colored crayon to draw around the lid.

3. Draw overlapping circles, repeating until the design looks full and pleasing.

4. Use crayons that complement each other to fill in the enclosed areas on the paper. Vary the colors, patterns, and textures.

5. Write in the artist's name and hang the drawing.

From *More Paper, Paint, and Stuff,* published by Scott, Foresman and Company. Copyright © 1989 Karen B. Kurtz and Mark A. Kurtz.

Crayon Easel

The Group Needs:

several floor-standing easels

large sheets of newsprint for the easel

crayons for the easel tray

Procedure:

Create seasonal or thematic pictures by drawing on the easel.

Variations:

1. This activity can be adapted to paint, wet chalk, or printing with paint techniques. Cover the working area with newspapers, and if paint is being used, make sure that smocks are handy.

2. This activity also can be adapted for use with different sizes of paper, including wallpaper or newspaper. When using smaller sizes of paper, however, place a larger piece of paper underneath to protect the easel before beginning the activity.

Rabbit

Each Child Needs:

one 12x18-inch sheet of pink, lavender, yellow, or light blue construction paper for the rabbit

three straws for the whiskers

crayons

scissors

The Group Needs:

construction paper scraps for details

stapler

Procedure:

1. Fold the construction paper in half, matching the short edges.

2. Cut along the fold line, making two pieces of paper each of which is about 9x12 inches.

3. Fold one of the 9x12-inch pieces in half, matching the short edges.

4. Beginning at the fold line, draw a large numeral "3" on the paper, ending back again at the fold line. Cut out the "3" and unfold. This makes the rabbit's head.

5. Use crayons to draw the eyes, whisker points, and mouth on the rabbit's head.

6. Cut into the fold line at the bottom of the head, stopping just below the rabbit's mouth. Fold the open edges together and staple shut. This makes a dimensional-looking chin.

7. Cut two long rabbit ears from the remaining piece of construction paper.

8. Glue the ears in place behind the head.

9. Cut the three straws in half and glue them to the whisker points for whiskers.

From *More Paper, Paint, and Stuff,* published by Scott, Foresman and Company. Copyright © 1989 Karen B. Kurtz and Mark A. Kurtz.

Reindeer

Advance Adult Preparation:

Use oaktag to prepare several copies of the antlers pattern on page 123.

Each Child Needs:

pattern for antlers, as above

one 4½x12-inch sheet of brown construction paper for the reindeer's head

two 4½x6-inch sheets of black construction paper for the antlers

crayons

scissors

glue

The Group Needs:

stapler

Procedure:

1. Lay the pattern on the black construction paper, draw around it, and cut out two antlers. Save the scraps.

2. Create the reindeer's face on the brown construction paper, using crayons or paper scraps to add facial accents: eyes, eyelashes, and a red nose. Place the facial features close together in the center of the paper.

3. Glue the antlers to the head. Position the antlers at the upper opposite corners of the brown construction paper, behind the front of the head.

4. Roll the reindeer's head into a circle, and staple the bottom corners of the paper together at the back.

5. Display.

From *More Paper, Paint, and Stuff,* published by Scott, Foresman and Company. Copyright © 1989 Karen B. Kurtz and Mark A. Kurtz.

Just Wishing

Advance Adult Preparation:

Collect, clean, and dry turkey wishbones.

Each Child Needs:

one turkey wishbone, as above

one 6x6-inch square of cardboard for the base

glue

scissors

The Group Needs:

assorted items like glitter, ribbons, feathers, buttons, egg carton sections, etc.

Procedure:

1. Glue the wishbone to the cardboard base and let dry.

2. Glue some of the assorted items to the wishbone. Try to vary the textures and patterns. The wishbone is finished when the effect looks pleasing to the child.

3. Allow the decorated wishbone to dry thoroughly.

From *More Paper, Paint, and Stuff,* published by Scott, Foresman and Company, Copyright © 1989 Karen B. Kurtz and Mark A. Kurtz.

Egg Paperweight

Advance Adult Preparation:

Collect plastic hosiery eggs.

Each Child Needs:

one plastic hosiery egg, as above

glue

The Group Needs:

red, blue, or gold glitter in shallow pans

clean sand in a container

plastic scoop or measuring cup

newspapers to cover working area

Procedure:

1. Measure about ¼ cup of sand into one half of the plastic egg.

2. Glue the halves of the egg together and let dry.

3. Apply glue to the outer surface of the egg, creating a design around the egg.

4. Working carefully, roll the egg in the glitter while the glue is still wet. When the egg is completely covered with glitter, shake off the excess.

5. Allow the egg to dry completely, and then use as a paperweight.

Variations:

1. To make a hanging ornament, attach a ribbon to the empty egg halves, and then glue together. Decorate as above.

2. Glue rickrack or scraps of fabric to the egg paperweight.

From More Paper, Paint, and Stuff, published by Scott, Foresman and Company. Copyright © 1989 Karen B. Kurtz and Mark A. Kurtz.

Martian

Advance Adult Preparation:

Prepare tempera paint for glossy surfaces. *See* page 111.

Each Child Needs:

one egg carton lid for the head

four egg carton sections for the bulging eyes and short legs

two pipe cleaners for the antennae

two small beads for the antennae tips

glue

scissors

The Group Needs:

orange, green, and purple tempera paint in small containers

brushes

newspapers for covering work area

Procedure:

1. Use scissors to poke two small holes into the Martian's head (egg carton lid) for the antennae.

2. Paint the head, eyes, and legs with tempera paint. Let dry.

3. Glue the eyes on top of the head and the legs underneath.

4. Attach the antennae through the holes in the head. If you want curled antennae, you can loop the pipe cleaners around your finger.

5. Glue beads to the antennae tips.

6. Attach the artist's name to the Martian and display.

From *More Paper, Paint, and Stuff*, published by Scott, Foresman and Company, Copyright © 1989 Karen B. Kurtz and Mark A. Kurtz.

Same Color Collage

Advance Adult Preparation:

Collect magazines that contain colored illustrations so that you can provide at least one magazine for each child.

Each Child Needs:

one or two magazines, as above

one 12x18-inch sheet of white construction paper for the background

glue

scissors

The Group Needs:

marker

Procedure:

1. Choose your favorite color. Then find pictures in the magazine(s) that contain your favorite color. Look for lighter and darker shades of the color.

2. Cut out these pictures and glue them to the background.

3. Use the marker to title the collage. Add the artist's name and display.

Wreath

Advance Adult Preparation:

Use oaktag to prepare several copies of the pattern on page 124.

Each Child Needs:

one 12x12-inch square of green construction paper for the wreath

three 1x12-inch strips of red construction paper for the ornaments

three 3x12-inch strips of white construction paper for the bow

one 3x3-inch square of white construction paper for the bow knot

pencil

glue

The Group Needs:

several patterns, as above

From *More Paper, Paint, and Stuff,* published by Scott, Foresman and Company. Copyright © 1989 Karen B. Kurtz and Mark A. Kurtz.

Procedure:

1. To make the wreath, start by folding the green construction paper in half.

2. Lay the pattern on the paper, matching the pattern's straight edges to the fold line, and draw around it.

3. With your fingers, carefully tear out the wreath along the line on the green paper.

4. To make an ornament, start by tearing one strip of red construction paper in half. Then form each strip into a circle and glue the ends together. Place one circle at a right angle inside the other circle and glue in place.

5. Repeat step 4 to create all three ornaments.

6. Now make the bow. Start by folding one strip of white construction paper in half and gluing the ends to create a loop. Repeat with another strip of white paper.

7. Overlap the glued ends of the two loops and glue together. Tear the remaining strip in half, making two shorter strips. Glue these strips underneath the loops.

8. To make the knot, round the corners on the white paper square to create a circle. Glue this circle over the loops of the bow.

9. Glue the knotted bow to the top of the wreath.

10. Arrange the ornaments around the wreath and glue in place.

From More Paper, Paint, and Stuff. published by Scott, Foresman and Company, Copyright © 1989 Karen B. Kurtz and Mark A. Kurtz.

Lion

Advance Adult Preparation:

Collect several books of wallpaper. Then, for each child, cut one large sheet of wallpaper into two smaller parts—one 9x12-inch sheet and one 4x4-inch square. Save all the scraps.

Each Child Needs:

one 9x12-inch sheet of wallpaper for the body

one 4x4-inch sheet of wallpaper for the face

scraps of wallpaper for the legs and tail

one 9x9-inch sheet of orange construction paper for the mane

pencil

scissors

glue

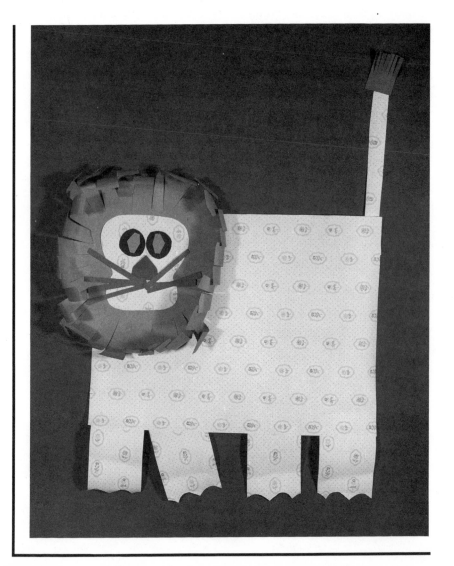

From *More Paper, Paint, and Stuff*, published by Scott, Foresman and Company. Copyright © 1989 Karen B. Kurtz and Mark A. Kurtz.

Procedure:

1. Use scissors to round the corners of the orange paper to make a circle.

2. Cut a fringe of about 1½ inches all around the circle. Then use a pencil to curl each piece of the fringe: curl the piece around the pencil, press, and release.

3. Glue the mane to one of the upper corners of the 9x12-inch sheet of wallpaper.

4. Fold the face paper in half. Then, with the fold in hand, cut an inverted pear shape from the paper and unfold. This is the lion's face.

5. Glue the face on top of the mane.

6. Cut facial features—eyes, nose, whiskers, tongue—from construction paper scraps. Glue in place.

7. From the wallpaper scraps, cut a long thin strip for the tail. Then glue the tail behind the body.

8. Use more construction paper scraps to create a fringe for the tail. Glue this fringe on top of the tail.

9. From the remaining wallpaper scraps, cut four legs; scallop one edge of each leg for the paw. Glue all four legs underneath the body.

Butterfly

Advance Adult Preparation:

Use oaktag to prepare several copies of the pattern on page 125.

Each Child Needs:

one 9x12-inch sheet of colored construction paper for the wings

one 3x9-inch sheet of black construction paper for the body

one black pipe cleaner for the antennae

crayons

glue

The Group Needs:

several butterfly patterns, as above

paper punch

Procedure:

1. Fold the paper in half, matching the short edges. Lay the oaktag pattern on the paper so that its straight edge matches the fold line.

2. Draw around the pattern on the paper and cut out the butterfly.

3. Unfold the butterfly. Use crayons to decorate its wings with colorful markings.

4. Use scissors to round the corners of the black paper so that you create an oval-shaped body for the butterfly.

5. Glue the body over the wings and let dry.

6. Cut the pipe cleaner in half to make two antennae.

7. Punch two holes in the head of the butterfly. Insert and secure each antenna through a hole, curling the tip with your fingers.

8. Attach the artist's name and display.

Variations:

1. Use colored tissue paper for the wings.

2. Use tempera paint for wing markings.

3. Glue scraps of construction paper to the wings for markings.

4. To make wings that sparkle, apply a thin line of glue around each wing and dip in glitter. Let dry thoroughly.

From *More Paper, Paint, and Stuff*, published by Scott, Foresman and Company. Copyright © 1989 Karen B. Kurtz and Mark A. Kurtz.

Paper Bag Pumpkin

Each Child Needs:

one lunch bag or grocery bag

one 9x12-inch sheet of green construction paper

scissors

The Group Needs:

lots of crumbled newspapers for stuffing

masking tape

orange tempera paint in small pans

newspapers for covering work area

brushes

Procedure:

1. Stuff the bag with newspapers.

2. Fold over the top of the bag and tape securely.

3. Paint the sides and top of the bag, and then allow it to dry.

4. Cut a large stem and one or two leaves out of the green construction paper. Glue in place.

Variations:

1. Pile paper bag pumpkins in the corner of the room. Connect them with a vine made of green construction paper chains and leaves.

2. Make a jack-o'-lantern by adding black tempera paint features. After step 3, paint a triangle nose, two triangle eyes, and a toothy grin. Allow to dry and complete with stem and leaves.

Orange

Each Child Needs:

one 16x24-inch sheet of newsprint

The Group Needs:

tempera paints—red, blue, yellow, white, and black—in small pans

brushes

water containers filled with water

newspapers for covering work area

Procedure:

1. Fold the paper in half, matching the short edges, and crease.

2. Fold the paper in half again, matching the long edges, and crease.

3. Unfold the paper completely.

4. Fold the paper in half, matching the long edges, and crease.

5. Fold the paper in half again, matching long edges, and crease.

6. Unfold the paper completely. It will now be divided into 16 rectangles.

7. Discuss how to make the color of orange with the group. Talk about how to keep the paints pure.

8. Have one child mix orange from red and yellow. Paint an orange shape in one of the rectangles.

9. Discuss how to make a different shade of orange. Children will discover they can change the shade by increasing or decreasing yellow and red, or by adding varying amounts of black or white.

10. Each child mixes his or her own orange color and paints shapes on the paper, filling all the rectangles.

11. Allow to dry.

Variations:

1. Hang each picture with the caption, "Orange is one, orange is many!"

2. Make sunrise or sunset pictures. After the paint has dried, cut out and glue on 12x18-inch drawing paper. Use crayons to complete the pictures.

3. Cut out leaf shapes from all the papers. Create an autumn tree and display.

From *More Paper, Paint, and Stuff,* published by Scott, Foresman and Company. Copyright © 1989 Karen B. Kurtz and Mark A. Kurtz.

Halloween Painting

Each Child Needs:

one sheet of newspaper

The Group Needs:

tempera paints—orange, black, and green—in small pans

brushes

newspapers for covering work area

Procedure:

1. Paint a Halloween picture on the newspaper. Ideas for such pictures include black cats, bats, witches, ghosts, pumpkins, and costumed children.

2. Dry, attach artist's name and title, and display the picture.

Printing

Each Child Needs:

one 9x12-inch sheet of construction paper

The Group Needs:

combs for printing

tempera paint (two or three colors)

newspapers for covering work area

Procedure:

1. Hold the comb in your hand, and dip it in paint.

2. Swirl the teeth of the comb on the paper, creating interesting designs.

3. Allow to dry.

Variations:

1. Have children create two paintings which, when dry, can be used as book covers.

2. Do all the paintings using just one color of paint. When they are dry, attach all of the papers to the wall. They will add interesting background texture and design.

3. Use other items for printing: e.g., cotton swabs, feathers, wooden or plastic spools. Fruits and vegetables cut in half also make excellent prints: e.g., green peppers with seed case intact, apples, grapefruit, pomegranates, pears, corn on the cob, mushrooms. Other natural items—seed pods, ferns, leaves, bark, and fossils—are also good. Discover your own possibilities!

From *More Paper, Paint, and Stuff*, published by Scott, Foresman and Company. Copyright © 1989 Karen B. Kurtz and Mark A. Kurtz.

Food Color Painting

Each Child Needs:

one white coffee filter

The Group Needs:

red, green, blue, and yellow food coloring

eye droppers

newspapers for covering work area

Procedure:

1. Fold and then unfold the coffee filter.

2. Use the eye droppers to drop food coloring onto the fold. Add food coloring to other places on the filter until the design looks pleasing.

3. Quickly fold the filter once again. The food coloring should soak and bleed through. Then unfold it.

4. Allow the food color paintings to dry, and then hang them in a window.

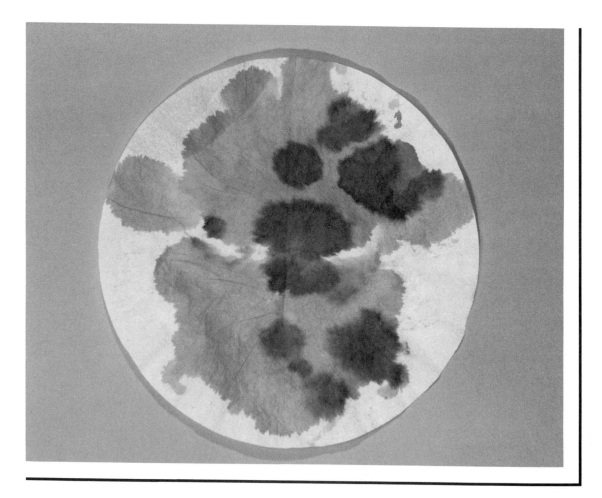

Blob

Each Child Needs:

one 9x12-inch sheet of construction paper

crayons

The Group Needs:

black tempera paint in a small container

brushes

newspapers for covering work area

Procedure:

1. Paint a blob anywhere on the paper and allow to dry.

2. What real object does the blob resemble? Use crayons to develop and complete the picture. Add accents.

3. Mat the picture and attach a title and the artist's name.

Variations:

1. Substitute a black construction paper circle for the black paint blob. Glue the circle to the paper, and then complete the picture with crayons as above.

2. Choose seasonal colors of paint and paper: red paper with green paint for Christmas, black paint with orange paper for Halloween, etc. Draw seasonal or thematic pictures.

3. Use other shapes—e.g., paisley swirl, straight line, wavy line, square, triangle, dot. Discover all the possibilities!

From *More Paper, Paint, and Stuff,* published by Scott, Foresman and Company, Copyright © 1989 Karen B. Kurtz and Mark A. Kurtz.

Stencil

Each Child Needs:

one 6x6-inch square of oaktag

one 9x12-inch sheet of construction paper

scissors

The Group Needs:

sponges, about 1x1-inch squares

tempera paint

Procedure:

1. Fold the oaktag in half, and cut a heart or other simple shape.

2. Unfold the oaktag, and lay the shape on the construction paper. Hold it securely in place with one hand.

3. With the other hand, dip the sponge into paint.

4. Stroke the sponge across the shape and onto the paper. Continue this procedure around all the edges of the design.

5. Carefully remove the oaktag shape and discard it.

6. Allow the stenciled design to dry, and then display.

Variations:

1. Substitute solid-colored fabric for the construction paper.

2. Use thinned acrylics instead of tempera paint.

The Sea

Advance Adult Preparation:

Use oaktag to prepare several copies of the patterns on page 126. If your group is unfamiliar with life in the sea, show a movie or read books from the library to introduce this project.

Each Child Needs:

one 16x24-inch sheet of fingerpaint paper for the sea

one 4x4-inch square of brown construction paper for the starfish

one 4x4-inch square of pink construction paper for the jellyfish

three 4x5-inch sheets assorted construction paper for the other fish

scissors

glue

crayons

The Group Needs:

several patterns, prepared as above

blue or green fingerpaint for underwater vegetation and rocks

construction paper scraps

large shallow pan of water

newspapers for covering work area

Procedure:

1. Discuss the world of the sea and the life in it: the kinds of animals, how they survive in the water, what colors and textures you might see underwater.

2. Dip the fingerpaint paper into water briefly.

3. Use your hand to paint sea weeds, other vegetation, and rocks on the fingerpaint paper. Create interesting effects with the side of your hand, your fist, and your fingers.

4. Allow the fingerpaint paper to dry.

5. Draw starfish, jellyfish, and other fish on the construction paper.

6. Cut out the sea creatures and glue to the fingerpaint seascape. Add other details—eyes, fins, tentacles—cut from construction paper scraps.

7. Add crayon accents to complete the seascape. Outline with black or dark brown crayon.

8. Attach the artist's name and display.

From *More Paper, Paint, and Stuff*, published by Scott, Foresman and Company, Copyright © 1989 Karen B. Kurtz and Mark A. Kurtz.

Strip Weaving

Each Child Needs:

one 9x12-inch sheet of construction paper for the weaving frame

scissors

The Group Needs:

1x9-inch strips of construction paper in assorted colors

Procedure:

1. Fold the frame paper in half, matching the short edges, and crease.

2. Use the scissors to make straight cuts from the fold line across to the opposite open edges of the paper, stopping about one inch from the edge. Cut in about one-inch intervals across the paper.

3. Unfold the paper. This makes the weaving frame.

4. Weave the strips of colored construction paper in and out across the frame. Weave the first strip over and under, over and under the frame. Weave the second strip under and over, under and over the frame. Repeat across the frame, alternating the weaving pattern as you work.

5. Push all the strips together securely so they will "lock" in place.

6. Attach the artist's name to the completed weaving and display.

Variations:

1. Make a weaving frame that has zigzag or scalloped lines instead of straight ones. Complete as above.

2. Use the woven mats as placemats for a party.

3. Use the woven mats as booklet covers.

From *More Paper, Paint, and Stuff*, published by Scott, Foresman and Company, Copyright © 1989 Karen B. Kurtz and Mark A. Kurtz.

Bright Wheel

Advance Adult Preparation:

Collect plastic lids from coffee cans, margarine tubs, or whipped topping containers.

Each Child Needs:

one plastic lid for the weaving
    frame, as above

yarn in assorted colors to weave

scissors

pencil

Procedure:

1. Use the scissors to cut away the rim from the lid.

2. Use the scissors or a pencil to poke a small hole in the center of the lid.

3. Cut five slits around the outside edge of the lid.

4. Tie yarn to one slit, then through the center hole. Fasten yarn onto each slit in a like manner until the lid looks like a wheel with spokes radiating out from the center. Knot each length of yarn securely.

5. Tie another long piece of yarn onto any spoke. Then use your fingers to weave the yarn over a spoke, under a spoke, over, under, and so on. Fasten on more yarn as needed and knot securely.

6. Weave on the other side of the wheel, if desired, by turning the lid over and repeating the procedure.

7. Suspend the decoration in a window or doorway.

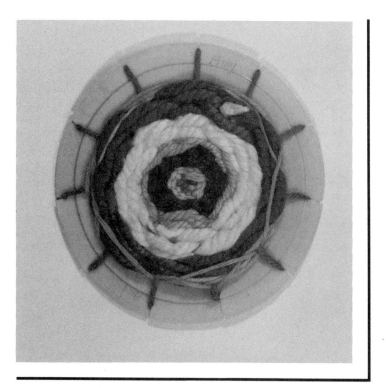

Hippo

Advance Adult Preparation:

Collect several books of wallpaper samples.

Each Child Needs:

one 9x18-inch sheet of yellow construction paper for the body

one 4x18-inch sheet of yellow construction paper for the legs

one 9x9-inch square of wallpaper for the head

scissors

glue

The Group Needs:

1x9-inch strips of construction paper in assorted colors

construction paper scraps

Procedure:

1. Fold the body paper in half, matching the short edges, and crease.

2. Beginning on the fold line, cut straight lines across to the opposite open edges, stopping about one inch from edge. Cut in about one-inch intervals across the paper.

3. Unfold the paper. This makes the weaving frame.

4. Weave the strips of colored construction paper in and out across the frame. Weave the first strip over and under, over and under the frame. Weave the second strip under and over, under and over the frame. Alternate the weaving pattern across the frame.

5. Push all the strips together securely so they "lock" against each other.

6. Glue all the ends of the strips to the back of the body paper.

7. Fold the face paper in half and crease. With your hand on the fold, cut a round, broad-looking hippo's face with little ears.

8. Glue the face to the top of the body.

9. Make accents—tiny eyes, inner ear marks—from construction paper scraps and glue in place.

10. Fold the leg paper in half, matching the short edges, and crease. Fold in half again, and then unfold. This gives you four legs for the hippo.

11. Cut the four legs apart on the fold lines. Glue the legs underneath the body.

12. Make a tiny tail for the hippo from construction paper scraps and glue in place.

13. Display.

Variation:

Substitute the hippo patterns on pages 127 and 128 for steps 1, 2, 7, and 10 above. Cut out the patterns and complete as above.

Coat Hanger Weaving

Advance Adult Preparation:

Collect wire coat hangers. Bend each hanger into a square by pulling on opposite corners. This makes the weaving frame.

Each Child Needs:

one coat hanger for weaving frame, prepared as above

scissors

yarn or heavy string

The Group Needs:

assorted items to weave: plastic bread wrappers (cut into 2-inch strips lengthwise); feathers; lightweight strips of rubber or wire; strips of textured fabric (cut into 4-inch strips lengthwise); buttons

Procedure:

1. Tie one end of a long piece of yarn or string to the wire frame.

2. Loop the yarn or string back and forth in about one-inch intervals across opposite sides of the frame. Each loop should wrap around the wire frame twice to secure it. Tie on more yarn as needed. Trim ends neatly. This completes the frame.

3. Choose an item to weave with, and tie it securely to the top of the frame. Trim off the end. Weave the item through the frame in an over-and-under pattern. When you need more weaving material, tie on another item and continue weaving. Press the woven materials together as you work. Weave until the design looks pleasing.

4. Knot and tie off the end of the weaving material, trimming it neatly.

5. Display the weaving by hanging it from its hook.

Variations:

1. Add tassels to the bottom edge of the weaving by attaching weaving strips. Let them hang down loosely.

2. Join several weavings together in a mobile. Hook or tie them onto each other, and then suspend all of them from another coat hanger.

From *More Paper, Paint, and Stuff*, published by Scott, Foresman and Company. Copyright © 1989 Karen B. Kurtz and Mark A. Kurtz.

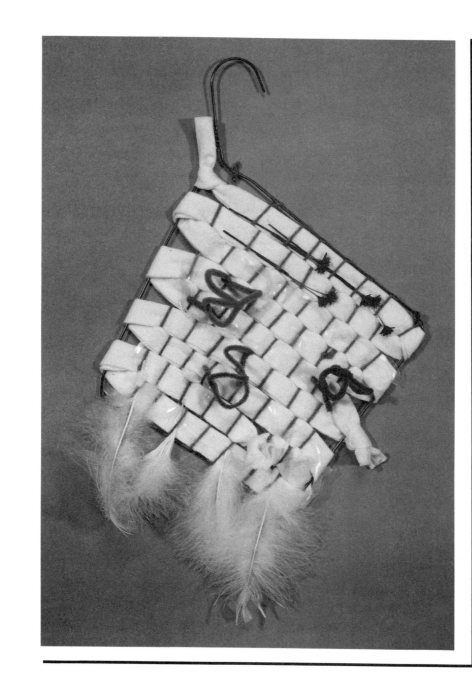

Shamrock

Advance Adult Preparation:

Use oaktag to prepare the pattern on page 129. Prepare a poem about the color green.

Each Child Needs:

one 9x12-inch sheet of green construction paper for the shamrock

1x9-inch strips of white construction paper for weaving

glue

scissors

pencil

The Group Needs:

several patterns, prepared as above

Procedure:

1. Fold the green construction paper in half, matching the short edges.

2. Lay the pattern on the paper, matching fold lines. Draw around the pattern and cut out the shamrock.

3. Weave the strips in and out, tightening them as you work so they "lock" against each other. Repeat until the weaving is completed.

4. Use scissors to trim the strips to fit the shamrock. Glue the woven strips in place on the back of the shamrock.

5. Read a poem about green, and then display the poem with the shamrocks.

From *More Paper, Paint, and Stuff*, published by Scott, Foresman and Company. Copyright © 1989 Karen B. Kurtz and Mark A. Kurtz.

Cardboard Weaving

Advance Adult Preparation:

Prepare weaving frames from 9x9-inch squares of lightweight cardboard. Cut one-inch slits on two opposite sides of the cardboard. Attach string to one end of the frame and knot it securely. Loop the string into slits across the frame, tying on more string if needed. Tie off the string when finished and trim the end. On the back of the frame, secure a strip of masking tape to hold the string in place.

Each Child Needs:

one cardboard weaving frame, prepared as above

The Group Needs:

rug yarn in assorted colors

Procedure:

1. Weave the yarn in an over-and-under pattern across the frame. Press the weaving together as you work.

2. When you finish, weave in the yarn ends between the yarn and frame.

3. Try to achieve interesting designs by using contrasting or complementary colors.

4. Display.

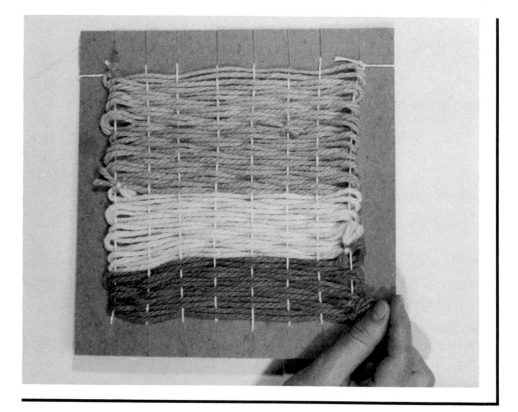

Basket

Each Child Needs:

six 1x12-inch strips of blue construction paper for the basket

six 1x12-inch strips of yellow construction paper for the basket

three 1x12-inch strips of blue or yellow construction paper for the handle and bows

The Group Needs:

stapler

Procedure:

1. Lay the blue strips on the work surface, keeping the ends even.

2. Weave in the yellow strips at right angles to the blue strips. Alternate the weaving pattern. Work the first strip over and under, over and under; work the second strip under and over, under and over. Keep all the ends even.

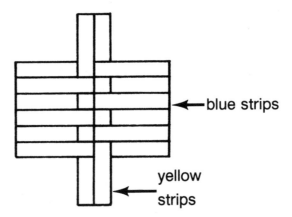

3. Press all the strips together so that they will "lock" in place.

4. Gather two sides of the basket in your hands. Staple together.

5. Repeat for the other two sides of the basket.

6. Using two more strips, staple a handle across the basket. Repeat for the other side.

7. Staple a bow at the top or sides of the basket.

Variations:

1. Fill the basket with nuts, candy, or other small snack foods. Small fresh flowers, dried seeds, or pinecones can also be used.

2. Vary the colors of the basket seasonally: orange and brown for autumn, red and green for Christmas, red and white or pink for Valentine's Day, green and white for Saint Patrick's Day.

3. Fill the basket and give it away to a friend.

From *More Paper, Paint, and Stuff*, published by Scott, Foresman and Company. Copyright © 1989 Karen B. Kurtz and Mark A. Kurtz.

Spider

Advance Adult Preparation:

Collect lightweight forked tree branches. Cut off the ends of the branches so they are even.

Each Child Needs:

one 2x2-inch square of black construction paper for the body of the spider

scissors

glue

The Group Needs:

yarn, in light colors for the web

assorted construction paper scraps for the spider

Procedure:

1. Make a weaving frame by knotting one end of the yarn to the branch. Trim the end of the yarn at the knot.

2. String the yarn across to the opposite fork of the branch. Then work the yarn back and forth, looping it around each fork. Continue in this manner out to the ends of the branch. Tie on more yarn as needed.

3. Knot the ends of the yarn securely and trim. This makes the weaving frame.

4. Knot one end of another long piece of yarn securely in the center of the frame and trim the end.

5. Make the web by weaving yarn in and out, over and under, or looping it around the frame. Tie on more yarn as needed, trimming the ends neatly as you work. Work outward from the center of the frame. Create an interesting design as you go, leaving some open spaces in the web, weaving densely in others. The web is finished when the design looks pleasing. Trim the end of the yarn.

6. Use scissors to round the corners of the black square. This makes the body of the fat spider.

7. Make eight legs from construction paper scraps and glue them underneath the body. Cut other scraps into geometric shapes and add to the body as accents.

8. Glue the spider to the web.

9. Display on a wall.

Variations:

1. Turn this into a cooperative activity. Working in small groups with a single large branch, the children weave a web and make a spider. Then they add other bugs caught in the web, creating the insects as they did the spider.

2. Substitute transparent monofilament fishing line for the yarn.

Candleholder

Advance Adult Preparation:

Collect used but clean tin cans. Remove the labels.

Each Child Needs:

one tin can, prepared as above

one small ball of florist's clay

one votive candle

The Group Needs:

large nails

hammers

acrylic paint in small containers

brushes

newspapers for covering work area

Procedure:

1. Use a hammer and nail to punch holes in the tin can. Work very carefully.

2. Paint the can and let it dry.

3. Anchor the clay ball inside the tin can at the center.

4. Anchor the candle in the clay ball.

From *More Paper, Paint, and Stuff*, published by Scott, Foresman and Company. Copyright © 1989 Karen B. Kurtz and Mark A. Kurtz.

Trivet

Advance Adult Preparation:

Collect ceramic tiles, each about 4½x4½ inches square.

Each Child Needs:

one ceramic tile, as above

The Group Needs:

acrylic paint, thinned, in small containers

small brushes

transparent spray lacquer

newspapers for covering work area

Procedure:

1. Paint a small design or picture on the tile, and allow to dry. Possible subjects for the painting include seasonal objects, vegetables, abstract designs, and hearts.

2. Spray the tile with two or three thin coatings of lacquer. Allow to dry thoroughly.

Variations:

1. Cover the back of the trivet with felt and glue in place.

2. Glue a small wooden bead underneath the trivet at each corner for legs.

From *More Paper, Paint, and Stuff.* published by Scott, Foresman and Company. Copyright © 1989 Karen B. Kurtz and Mark A. Kurtz.

Valentine Packet

Each Child Needs:

one 12x18-inch sheet of red construction paper for the packet

scissors

glue

The Group Needs:

assorted items to decorate the packet: wallpaper, paper doilies, glitter, yarn

construction paper scraps for decorating

stapler

Procedure:

1. Fold the red construction paper, matching short edges. Stop about one inch from the edge.

2. Staple the edges of the construction paper. This creates the packet.

3. Decorate the front of the packet. The design is finished when it looks pleasing.

4. Make valentines or notes to put inside the packet, and give it as a gift to someone you love.

Variation:

Use oaktag to prepare the pattern on page 130. Lay the pattern on construction paper, draw around it, and cut it out. This gives you the heart shape for making valentines. Decorate the valentines and place inside the packet.

From More Paper, Paint, and Stuff, published by Scott, Foresman and Company. Copyright © 1989 Karen B. Kurtz and Mark A. Kurtz.

Bookmark

Advance Adult Preparation:

Collect clean white envelopes and used greeting cards.

Each Child Needs:

one white envelope, as above

glue

scissors

The Group Needs:

greeting cards, as above

Procedure:

1. Cut a corner from the envelope. This makes the bookmark.

2. Paste a design or picture cut from a greeting card over the bookmark.

3. Slip the bookmark over several pages in a book.

Notecards

Advance Adult Preparation:

Press flowers or weeds between the pages of an old catalog for about one or two weeks. Collect white envelopes, each about 5x6 inches.

Each Child Needs:

four 6x9-inch sheets of white construction paper for the notecards

two white facial tissues for decorating the notecards

four white envelopes, as above, large enough to hold the notecards

one plastic sandwich bag, slightly larger than the notecards

glue

scissors

The Group Needs:

flowers or weeds, prepared as above

thinned glue and water mixture in small containers

brushes

newspapers for covering work area

Procedure:

1. Fold the white construction paper in half, matching the short edges. When folded, the paper will measure about 4½x6 inches. Crease the fold. This makes a notecard. Repeat for each notecard.

2. Arrange one to five pressed flowers or weeds in an interesting design on the front of each notecard. Touch with glue to anchor the decoration in place, and allow to dry.

3. Unfold the notecards. Then separate each facial tissue and lay a one-ply thickness over the front of the notecard. Gently paint over the one-ply tissue with the thinned glue and water mixture. Allow to dry thoroughly.

4. Use scissors to trim the tissue from the edges of the notecard. Dry thoroughly, if needed.

5. Assemble the notecards and envelopes.

6. Place the stationery in the plastic bag and seal.

From *More Paper, Paint, and Stuff*, published by Scott, Foresman and Company. Copyright © 1989 Karen B. Kurtz and Mark A. Kurtz.

Tannenbaum

Advance Adult Preparation:

Use oaktag to prepare the pattern on page 131. Cut out two shapes for each tree from green felt. Cut old but clean pantyhose into small pieces.

Each Child Needs:

two green felt tree shapes, prepared as above

one large star-shaped sequin

glue

scissors

yarn

The Group Needs:

large-eyed tapestry needles

pieces of pantyhose, prepared as above

small sequins

glitter

buttons

rickrack

Procedure:

1. Match the two tree pieces. Use needle and yarn to sew up the two sides of the tree.

2. Stuff the tree lightly with pieces of pantyhose.

3. Sew up the bottom of the tree.

4. Glue decorations to the front of the tree: sequins, glitter, rickrack, buttons.

5. Glue a star at the top of the tree.

Star Magnet

Advance Adult Preparation:

Use oaktag to prepare the pattern on page 132. Cut out one star shape from lightweight yellow cardboard.

Each Child Needs:

one cardboard star, prepared as above

glue

small magnet

The Group Needs:

buttons, small pieces of old jewelry, or school picture

Procedure:

1. Glue the buttons, jewelry, or picture to the front of the star. Allow to dry.
2. Glue the magnet to the back of the star, and allow to dry.

From *More Paper, Paint, and Stuff,* published by Scott, Foresman and Company. Copyright © 1989 Karen B. Kurtz and Mark A. Kurtz.

Bracelet

Advance Adult Preparation:

Collect pieces of colored Velcro material (fuzzy-side up), about 1 or 1½ inches wide. Collect small novelty buttons, small wooden cutouts, or old earrings with flat backs (clips removed) for use as bracelet decorations.

Each Child Needs:

one strip of colored Velcro, as above, sized to fit wrist and allowing 2 inches of overlap

one ½x½-inch square of Velcro (looped-side up)

one ½x1½-inch piece of Velcro (looped-side up)

glue

one decoration, as above

Procedure:

1. Cut the Velcro strip to fit the wrist, allowing about two inches of overlap.

2. Glue the ½x½-inch square of Velcro underneath the bracelet decoration.

3. Press the decoration against the center of the bracelet.

4. Glue the ½x1½-inch piece of Velcro underneath one end of the bracelet. Allow to dry.

5. Attach the bracelet to the wrist.

Variation:

Use the same procedure to make belts instead of bracelets.

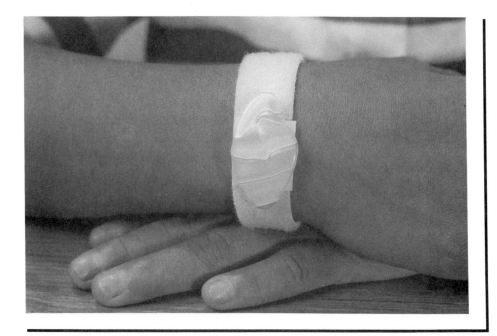

From *More Paper, Paint, and Stuff*, published by Scott, Foresman and Company. Copyright © 1989 Karen B. Kurtz and Mark A. Kurtz.

Dye a Dozen

Advance Adult Preparation:

Collect dry onion skins. Buy a dozen eggs.

The Group Needs:

eggs and onion skins, as above

string or heavy rug yarn for wrapping
around the eggs

saucepan filled with water and a lid

hot plate

bowl

Procedure:

1. Tie the string carefully around an egg. Crisscross the string around and over the egg several times. Tie off the ends securely.

2. Place the dry onion skins in the saucepan. Add the string-wrapped eggs. Cover with water.

3. Cover the eggs with more onion skins, placing some of the skins between the eggs.

4. Place the lid on the saucepan, and put the saucepan on the hot plate. Cook the eggs slowly on low heat until they are hard-boiled.

5. Drain off the skins and water. When the eggs have cooled, cut off the strings.

6. Enjoy the designs—then eat!

Variations:

1. Wrap an egg with a small green leaf, secure the leaf with string, and then hard-boil the egg.

2. Substitute thick rubber bands for the string.

From *More Paper, Paint, and Stuff,* published by Scott, Foresman and Company. Copyright © 1989 Karen B. Kurtz and Mark A. Kurtz.

Heirlooms

Each Child Needs:

one family heirloom, small enough to be hand-carried and preferably smaller than a 12x18-inch sheet of drawing paper

one 12x18-inch sheet of white drawing paper

crayons

The Group Needs:

masking tape to anchor the heirloom to the paper

marking pen

Procedure:

1. Discuss the meaning of a family heirloom.

2. On a designated day, have the children bring the heirlooms. Small books, snapshots, old lace collars, or antique toys would all be good for this activity. The children should be prepared to share their heirlooms with the group and to tell about each object's importance to their family.

3. Use crayons to create a picture about the heirloom on the drawing paper.

4. Tape the drawing paper to the heirloom.

5. Put a title on the picture and display it.

Older Friends

Advance Adult Preparation:

Prepare the list of questions suggested in step 2.

Each Child Needs:

one 9x12-inch sheet of drawing paper

one 9x12-inch sheet of writing paper

crayons

pencil

Procedure:

1. Talk with the group about the oldest people they know. Discuss how older generations lived, played, and worked, and what new inventions they experienced during their lifetimes.

2. Have the children interview the oldest people they know. An adult can help ask the questions and take notes, or the children can tape the interview and play it back later. Here is a suggested list of questions for the children to ask:

   What did you like to do most when you were my age?

   What did you like to do most in school?

   Can you tell me about a gift you received when you were very young?

   What was your favorite toy when you were young?

   What is the earliest event in history that you remember?

   When you were young, what did you want to grow up to be?

   What is your most treasured possession?

   What do you like to do most now?

3. Discuss the interviews together. Write a story about the interview and draw a picture to illustrate it.

Variations:

1. Children share their stories with the interviewees.

2. Compile the stories into a book.

3. Type the stories and have the children take them home to read.

4. Display the stories and illustrations.

From *More Paper, Paint, and Stuff,* published by Scott, Foresman and Company. Copyright © 1989 Karen B. Kurtz and Mark A. Kurtz.

Paper Punch Designs

Each Child Needs:

one 9x12-inch sheet of colored construction paper for the design

one 9x12-inch sheet of white construction paper for the background

glue

The Group Needs:

paper punch

Procedure:

1. Fold the colored construction paper in half, matching the short edges.

2. Beginning at the fold, cut a simple shape (a heart, star, or flower) from the paper.

3. Unfold the paper.

4. Use the paper punch to punch holes all around the edges of the shape.

5. Refold the paper and punch holes in the inside of the shape.

6. Glue the paper to the background.

Variations:

1. Prepare the simple heart, tree, and star patterns from pages 130, 131, and 132. Lay each pattern on folded colored construction paper, matching the fold line. Draw around and cut out. Complete as above, beginning with step 3.

2. Substitute lightweight foil for the colored construction paper.

3. Substitute colored tissue paper for the colored construction paper.

From *More Paper, Paint, and Stuff,* published by Scott, Foresman and Company. Copyright © 1989 Karen B. Kurtz and Mark A. Kurtz.

Reverse Glass Painting

Advance Adult Preparation:

Collect aluminum foil and small plastic picture frames with glass covers and cardboard backs. Clean the glass covers.

Each Child Needs:

one small picture frame with glass cover and cardboard back, as above

one 12x12-inch sheet of aluminum foil

The Group Needs:

acrylic paints in assorted colors in small containers, thinned enough to be transparent when applied

small brushes

newspapers to cover working area

Procedure:

1. On the back of the glass cover, paint one simple design (like a flower, bird, egg, heart, or tree). Add a few simple painted accents: eye and beak for the bird, spirals on the egg, trunk on the tree. Leave some unpainted spaces on the glass. Allow to dry. This completes the reverse glass design.

2. Crumble the aluminum foil, and then wrap it around the cardboard back. Use tape, if necessary, to secure the edges of the foil to the back.

3. Slip the glass cover with the design inside into the picture frame.

4. Place the foil-covered back into the frame behind the painted glass. Anchor securely.

5. Display. The aluminum foil will show through the unpainted spaces on the glass.

From *More Paper, Paint, and Stuff,* published by Scott, Foresman and Company. Copyright © 1989 Karen B. Kurtz and Mark A. Kurtz.

Tin Punch Star

Advance Adult Preparation:

Use oaktag to prepare the star pattern on page 132.

Each Child Needs:

one aluminum pie plate or square tray, about 8 inches

marker

scissors

glue

The Group Needs:

several star patterns, prepared as above

several large nails

several hammers

glitter in a shallow pan

hard-surfaced work area for punching out designs

Procedure:

1. Lay the star pattern on the pie plate, draw around it with a marker, and cut it out. Straighten the edges of the star if necessary.

2. For the punched-tin look, use a marker to make small dots on the star. The more area that is punched out, the more attractive the final result.

3. Lay the star on a hard surface. Using a hammer and nail, very carefully punch through the marked dots.

4. To decorate the star, run a fine line of glue around the edges and dip in glitter. Shake off any excess glitter.

Doll

Advance Adult Preparation:

Collect old solid-colored bed sheets or muslin. Use oaktag to prepare the pattern on page 133.

Each Child Needs:

one piece of bed sheet or muslin about 9x24 inches

pencil

fabric crayons

The Group Needs:

iron

large-eyed tapestry needles

yarn

scissors

pieces of pantyhose or polyester stuffing for the doll

newspapers for pressing crayons into the fabric

Procedure:

1. Fold the fabric in half, matching the short edges.

2. Press on the fold line with a warm iron.

3. Lay the pattern on the fabric, draw around it, and cut out both pieces to make the front and back of the doll.

4. Use fabric crayons to decorate the front and back of the doll. Add accents: clothing, hair, facial features. Press the crayons heavily onto the fabric.

5. Separate the two pieces of fabric and lay each face-up on newspaper.

6. Cover each piece of fabric with another piece of newspaper. Glide a warm iron slowly over both the front and back of the doll. This process will set the crayons into the fabric.

7. Remove the newspapers.

8. Match the front to the back of the doll.

9. Thread yarn into the needles.

10. With the crayoned-sides of the doll out, sew around it, matching the edges as you work. Keep one side of the doll—along a shoulder or leg—open. Attach more yarn as needed. Trim the ends neatly.

11. Stuff the doll.

12. Sew the open side of the doll shut.

13. Display.

From *More Paper, Paint, and Stuff*, published by Scott, Foresman and Company. Copyright © 1989 Karen B. Kurtz and Mark A. Kurtz.

Quilt

Advance Adult Preparation:

Collect old solid-colored bed sheets. Prepare a powdered milk solution according to the recipe on the powdered milk container. Dip the sheets in the solution. Allow to dry. Then cut the sheets into pieces of about 12x18 inches.

Each Child Needs:

one piece of bed sheet, prepared as above   chalk in assorted colors

black or other dark-colored chalk

Procedure:

1. Use the black chalk to draw horizontal lines across the sheet in about 3- or 4-inch intervals.

2. Repeat the process, drawing vertical lines across the sheet in the same manner. The lines divide the quilt into patches.

3. Use the assorted chalk to color in each patch. Some of the patches can be solid-colored, but others should have lines, squiggles, or designs in them. Plan ahead so that colors which are compatible and complementary are near each other.

4. Display the quilt on the wall.

Variations:

1. If old bed sheets are not available, use white drawing paper and complete the quilt with crayons.

2. Decorate the quilt by using the wet chalk technique. Briefly dip sheets of white drawing paper into a shallow pan of water. Then use colored chalk to create the designs.

3. Instead of pre-treating the sheets in the powdered milk solution, you can run a warm iron over the crayoned designs to set them. Be sure to place newspaper over the fabric before ironing.

From *More Paper, Paint, and Stuff*, published by Scott, Foresman and Company. Copyright © 1989 Karen B. Kurtz and Mark A. Kurtz.

Eggs in a Basket

Advance Adult Preparation:

Create a large basket from a sheet of brown paper, about 3x4 feet. First, fold and crease the paper in half, matching the short edges. Then, beginning at the fold line, cut rounded lines to form the top and bottom of the basket. Go back to the fold line and cut straight lines across the basket lengthwise, stopping about two inches from the edge. Unfold the paper; this completes the weaving frame.

Weave 2x36-inch strips of brown paper over and under the frame. Trim and glue the ends to the back of the basket. Staple a handle, about 2x60 inches, across the top of the basket. Staple the basket to the wall display, leaving the rim open for placing eggs inside.

Each Child Needs:

one 9x12-inch sheet of white drawing paper

pencil

scissors

The Group Needs:

watercolors

brushes

small containers filled with water

newspapers for covering work area

Procedure:

1. Use a pencil to draw an egg shape on the paper.

2. Cut out the shape.

3. Decorate the egg with watercolors. Use straight, wavy, or scalloped lines, geometric shapes, or create a realistic picture. Keep the watercolors pure by dipping the brushes in water often.

4. Allow the egg to dry.

5. Staple the eggs inside the basket.

6. Attach a poem about Easter eggs near the display.

From *More Paper, Paint, and Stuff*, published by Scott, Foresman and Company, Copyright © 1989 Karen B. Kurtz and Mark A. Kurtz.

Clothespin Creatures

Advance Adult Preparation:

Collect non-spring clothespins and small, plastic googly eyes to be used for the butterflies.

Each Child Needs:

one clothespin, as above, for the body

one 9x9-inch square of colored tissue paper or reversible gift
   wrap for the wings

two googly eyes, as above

one short bag tie for antennae

glue

scissors

pencil

The Group Needs:

tempera paint in small containers

small brushes

newspapers for covering work area

Procedure:

1. Paint the clothespin and let it dry.

2. Glue the googly eyes in place at the head-end of the butterfly.

3. Glue the bag tie to the head to make antennae.

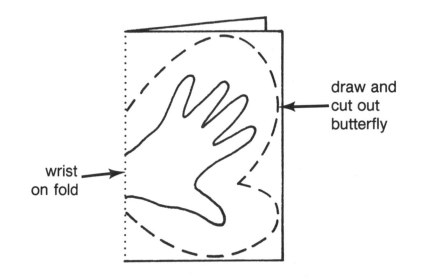

wrist
on fold

draw and
cut out
butterfly

From *More Paper, Paint, and Stuff*, published by Scott, Foresman and Company, Copyright © 1989 Karen B. Kurtz and Mark A. Kurtz.

4. To make the butterfly wings, fold the tissue paper or gift wrap in half. Place a wrist on the fold line, and lay hand along the fold; draw around it. Cut out both wings, leaving the fold intact.

5. Open the paper and crumple it together loosely at the fold.

6. Glue the wings to the top of the clothespin.

7. Display the clothespin creatures on lightweight tree branches, pussywillows, or cattails. Attach the poem "Fuzzy Wuzzy, Creepy Crawly" by Lillian Schulz near the display.

Variations:

1. To make a caterpillar, do steps 1, 2, and 3, but do not add wings.

2. To make a dragonfly, do steps 1, 2, and 3. Then use wide lace or ribbon to make a double bow tie for the wings. Glue in place. Complete with step 7 as above.

Fine Art Slides

Advance Adult Preparation:

From a fine arts museum or library, obtain 35 mm color transparencies (slides) of about 36 to 48 famous paintings. Have a slide projector and a screen ready for viewing.

Each Child Needs:

one 9x12-inch sheet of drawing paper

crayons

The Group Needs:

slides, projector, and screen, as above

Procedure:

1. Show the slides to the group.

2. Let each child pick a favorite and draw a picture of the painting.

3. Attach the names of both the painter and the child to the picture. Display.

From *More Paper, Paint, and Stuff,* published by Scott, Foresman and Company, Copyright © 1989 Karen B. Kurtz and Mark A. Kurtz.

Early Days Exhibit

Each Child Needs:

one or several antiques, small enough to carry in the hands

one 9x12-inch sheet of drawing paper

crayons

Procedure:

1. On a designated day, have the children bring in at least one antique. They should be prepared to tell about the history of their object, how their family came to own it, or why the object was useful in earlier days.

2. Children share their heirlooms with the group.

3. Assemble all the antiques on a display table. Place a sign with the name of each item near the antique.

4. Children draw a picture of their favorite item and make up a description of it. An adult can write the description on the drawing paper.

5. Display all the pictures together in a book.

Exchange Box

Advance Adult Preparation:

Arrange a mutual exchange with a group in a different geographical area or country. Ask the children to bring in one nonreturnable object to share—e.g., a snapshot, favorite drawing, small crafts, small items from nature, pencils.

The Group Needs:

collected objects, as above

a box for mailing

3x6-inch strips of paper for captions

Procedure:

1. Children share their objects with the group.

2. Children write a caption and attach it to the object.

3. Package the objects and mail them to a group in a different location.

4. When the other sends its own package to your group, allow the children to open and enjoy the surprises! Keep the items for an exhibit or share them at home or with another group. Write thank you letters to your group's new friends.

From *More Paper, Paint, and Stuff,* published by Scott, Foresman and Company. Copyright © 1989 Karen B. Kurtz and Mark A. Kurtz.

Opportunity Box

Each Child Needs:

one shoe box with lid

crayons

clay

other items that can be added to the box periodically: yarn, glitter, buttons, pinecones, smooth rocks

Procedure:

1. Place the crayons and clay in the box. Explain how the box and the items in it can be used during free time to create pictures on drawing paper or construction paper. Suggest that the children bring their own seasonal or thematic objects to add to their boxes periodically.

2. Provide "creating" time.

3. Encourage the children to share their creations with others.

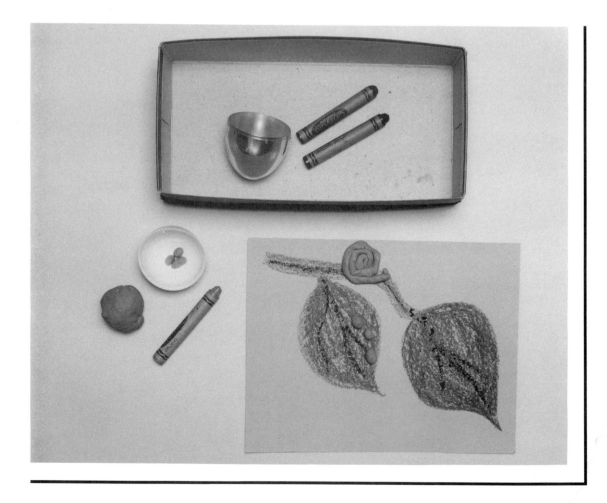

Sound Circle

Each Child Needs:

one 12x12-inch sheet of yellow
   construction paper for the circle

one old magazine

scissors

pencil

glue

Procedure:

1. Use scissors to round off the corners of the paper, making a circle.

2. Fold the circle in half. Then repeat this process twice more so that the circle, when unfolded, has eight sections.

3. Use a pencil to draw a line on each fold line.

4. Label each section of the circle with a consonant or sound symbol.

5. Find pictures in the magazine that have the same beginning sounds. Cut out and glue the pictures in place until the circle is full of sound pictures.

Variations:

1. Adapt the activity to ending sounds, numbers, colors, addition facts, etc.

2. If old magazines are not available, use crayons to draw pictures on the circle.

From *More Paper, Paint, and Stuff*, published by Scott, Foresman and Company. Copyright © 1989 Karen B. Kurtz and Mark A. Kurtz.

Word Building

Each Child Needs:

one 9x12-inch sheet of oaktag for the folder

15 2½x2½-inch squares of oaktag for the cards

scissors

crayons

stapler

Procedure:

1. Fold up about two inches on the sheet of oaktag along one long edge. Crease.

2. Staple along the folded line at three equal intervals. This completes the word building folder.

3. Use crayons to write one of the following letters on each card: t, e, n, b, l, f, p, d, a, i, o, u, s, m, c.

4. Place the cards into the folder. Then make a word by pulling out two, three, or four letters. Say the word aloud after it is formed. Use the word aloud in a sentence.

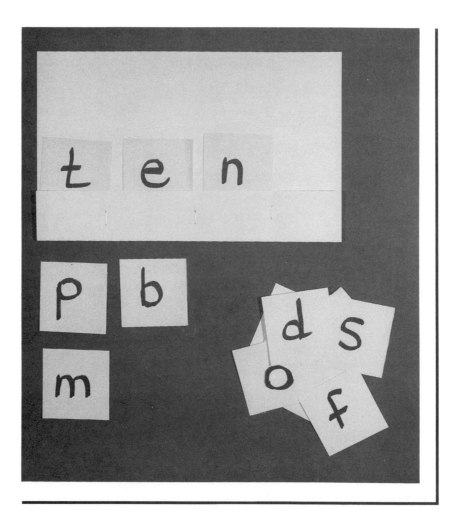

Water Play

Advance Adult Preparation:

Collect two large plastic dishpans and an assortment of plastic utensils: cups, spoons, small bowls, sieves, strainers, glasses, and lids.

The Group Needs:

one plastic dishpan, as above, half filled with water

one plastic dishpan, as above, empty

plastic utensils, as above

dishwashing liquid

plastic to cover working area

towels

Procedure:

1. Add several drops of dishwashing liquid to the dishpan half filled with water.

2. Place the plastic utensils in the dishpan.

3. Demonstrate measuring, filling, and emptying the utensils.

Variations:

1. Substitute marbles or clean, smooth rocks for the plastic utensils.

2. Tint the water with several drops of food coloring.

3. Sort objects by demonstrating whether they sink or float in the water.

From *More Paper, Paint, and Stuff*, published by Scott, Foresman and Company. Copyright © 1989 Karen B. Kurtz and Mark A. Kurtz.

Five-Pointed Star

Each Child Needs:

one 9x12-inch sheet of colored tissue paper for the star

scissors

Procedure:

1. Fold the tissue paper in half, matching the short edges.

2. Fold the top of the paper down to the bottom of the paper. The upper left corner will form a point on the bottom edge of the paper. This makes the second fold.

3. Fold the left side up over second fold. This makes the third fold.

4. Fold the top down over third fold.

5. While holding the point of the paper in your hand, cut off the point diagonally.

6. Unfold the tissue paper.

From *More Paper, Paint, and Stuff*, published by Scott, Foresman and Company. Copyright © 1989 Karen B. Kurtz and Mark A. Kurtz.

Thought Book

Advance Adult Preparation:

Prepare journals by stapling construction paper covers to several sheets of writing paper. Label each journal, "My Thought Book."

Each Child Needs:

one journal, prepared as above

pencil

Procedure:

1. Discuss the types of personal journal entries that may be included in the book: copying favorite poems, writing original poems, handwriting assignments (letters, numbers), writing names, making lists, creating original stories. The child's level of writing will depend on his or her age and maturity. The writing should focus on enjoyable experiences and feelings.

2. Provide "writing and creating" time. This activity is a good one for free-time opportunities. Keep the journals in an easily accessible place and keep on writing!

Variations:

1. Periodically, a child can pick one part of his or her journal to read and share with a friend. Adults should check the journals periodically.

2. Children may choose to illustrate their journals with pictures cut from magazines and glued in place, or they may use crayons to create their own original pictures.

From *More Paper, Paint, and Stuff*, published by Scott, Foresman and Company. Copyright © 1989 Karen B. Kurtz and Mark A. Kurtz.

Letters

Advance Adult Preparation:

Arrange for mutual pen pals with local friends or children in another state or country.

Each Child Needs:

one 9x12-inch sheet of writing paper

one envelope

one first-class postage stamp

pencil

Procedure:

1. Discuss these questions: "What do you like to read in a letter? What interesting things could you share about yourself? Your family? Your life?" Encourage children to give specific examples about their pets, vacations, sports, school, or celebrations of special days. With younger children, you may choose to write a dictated group letter. Older children can write their own letters.

2. Children write their letters. Then they address and stamp their envelopes.

3. Mail the letters.

4. When the responses arrive, the children read the letters from their pen pals. They may want to share highlights with others in the group. Children may take their letters home to share with their families.

Alphabet Cards

Advance Adult Preparation:

Use oaktag or white construction paper to prepare 26 cards, each cut from a 3-inch square of paper. Use a marking pen to draw one letter of the alphabet on each card.

Each Child Needs:

one set of alphabet cards, prepared as above

one 9x12-inch sheet of colored construction paper for the packet

crayons

scissors

The Group Needs:

stapler

Procedure:

1. To prepare the alphabet card packet, fold one edge of the colored construction paper up to about one inch of the top, matching the short edges. Crease the fold line.

2. Staple the sides of the packet together securely.

3. Place the alphabet cards inside the packet for storage.

4. To play the game, arrange the cards in the correct sequence so that vowels and consonants make words.

Variation:

Use numbers and number symbols instead of letters on the cards. Then use the cards for doing simple arithmetic problems.

From *More Paper, Paint, and Stuff*, published by Scott, Foresman and Company. Copyright © 1989 Karen B. Kurtz and Mark A. Kurtz.

Snowy Thoughts

Each Child Needs:

one 12x18-inch sheet of white drawing paper

crayons

Procedure:

1. After the first snowfall of the year, discuss snowy thoughts. Ask: "What snowy thoughts are in your mind?"

2. Draw a head on the paper. Add facial features: freckles, glasses, eyelashes, eyebrows.

3. Draw a line across the forehead, separating the forehead from the rest of the face. In the upper forehead area, draw your snowy thoughts. Complete with details.

Variations:

1. Discuss the picture with others.

2. Write a story about the picture.

3. Adapt the activity for other seasons or themes.

Octopus Game

Advance Adult Preparation:

Collect small paper plates.

Each Child Needs:

one paper plate, as above, for the octopus

two flat buttons

eight pieces of yarn, each about 12 inches long, for tentacles

crayons

scissors

glue

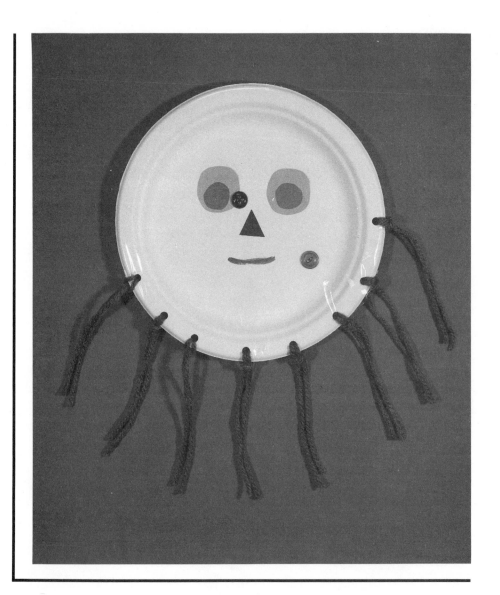

From *More Paper, Paint, and Stuff*. published by Scott, Foresman and Company. Copyright © 1989 Karen B. Kurtz and Mark A. Kurtz.

The Group Needs:

construction paper scraps

paper punch

plastic wrap to cover the octopus

masking tape

Procedure:

1. Create two eyes and a nose for the octopus from construction paper scraps. Glue them in place on the plate. Allow to dry.

2. Use a crayon to draw a mouth.

3. Lay the buttons on the octopus, and then seal the entire plate with plastic wrap. Tape the plastic wrap securely to the back of the plate.

4. Punch eight holes near the bottom edge of the plate. String yarn into holes and knot. This completes the octopus.

5. To play the game, two or more players take turns jiggling their plates. If the two buttons land on eyes, the player scores five points; if just one button lands on an eye, the player scores two points. The first player to score ten points is the winner.

Wind Flag

Advance Adult Preparation:

Collect clean plastic bread wrappers and dowel rods, about 18 inches long.

Each Child Needs:

one bread wrapper, as above, for the flag

one dowel rod, as above, for the pole

scissors

The Group Needs:

masking tape

Procedure:

1. Tape the short sides of the bread wrapper along the length of the dowel rod. Reinforce securely.

2. Cut one-inch strips lengthwise into the bread wrapper, stopping about two inches from the tape.

3. Place the wind flag in the ground.

4. Observe the wind direction.

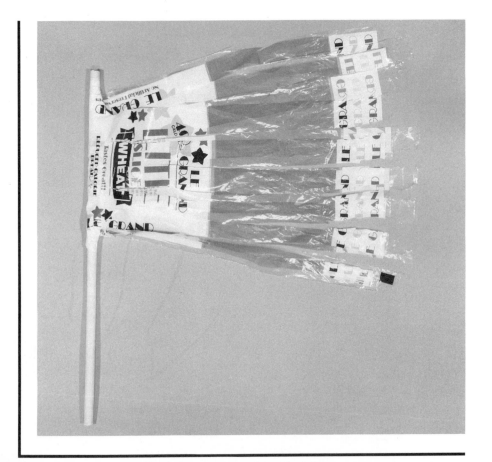

From *More Paper, Paint, and Stuff*, published by Scott, Foresman and Company. Copyright © 1989 Karen B. Kurtz and Mark A. Kurtz.

Train

Each Child Needs:

several 4x9-inch sheets of white construction paper for cars in the train

crayons

scissors

The Group Needs:

3x3-inch squares of black construction paper for wheels of the train car

masking tape

Procedure:

1. On one sheet of white paper, draw a train car, using a crayon to add accents. This makes one car for the train. Use as many sheets of white paper as you want cars.

2. Cut rounded corners from two black squares to make wheels for the train car. Glue them underneath the car. This completes one train car with wheels. Use as many wheels, in pairs, as there are cars in the train.

3. Turn the cars over. Connect the cars together by taping them along the short edges. This turns the separate cars into a train.

4. Run the train up and down or stand it up in a display.

Variations:

1. Make a circus train. Use crayons to draw animals and trainers. Glue black construction paper strips over each car to look like vertical bars in animal cages.

2. Make a train that carries coal, automobiles, fuel, groceries, etc.

3. Glue construction paper cut-outs in each car.

From *More Paper, Paint, and Stuff*, published by Scott, Foresman and Company, Copyright © 1989 Karen B. Kurtz and Mark A. Kurtz.

Van Gogh's Sunflowers

Advance Adult Preparation:

Obtain a print of Van Gogh's ''Sunflowers.'' Display the print in the room.

Each Child Needs:

one 12x18-inch sheet of yellow construction paper for sunflowers

The Group Needs:

orange, yellow, brown, green, and black colored chalk

shallow pan of water

newspapers to cover working area

From *More Paper, Paint, and Stuff*, published by Scott, Foresman and Company. Copyright © 1989 Karen B. Kurtz and Mark A. Kurtz.

Procedure:

1. Briefly discuss the life of Vincent Van Gogh. Point out the location of his homeland, the Netherlands, on a map. Discuss his painting of "Sunflowers." Here are some possible questions you might ask: "How does the picture make you feel? What colors did Van Gogh use? How did he achieve a happy feeling in this picture? Do all the sunflowers face the light?"

2. Dip the construction paper in water briefly.

3. Use various colored chalks to draw sunflowers on the paper. Fill the paper with sunflowers!

4. Allow the wet chalk drawing to dry.

5. Attach the child's name to the drawing and display.

Variation:

Adapt this wet chalk technique, which will not smear, to other activities.

Birthday Celebration

Advance Adult Preparation:

Obtain the ingredients to make a birthday cake with frosting. For this activity, you can use either a box mix or fresh ingredients.

The Group Needs:

cake to make and bake, as above

knife for frosting and cutting cake

plastic spoons

small plastic plates

newspapers to cover working area

Procedure:

1. Make and bake the birthday cake.

2. When the cake has cooled, frost it.

3. Cut the cake into slices, serve on the plastic plates, and enjoy!

Variations:

1. Have the birthday child (or children) make the cake for all.

2. Have several of the best friends of the honored child (children) make the cake.

3. Have the entire group, except the birthday child, make the special surprise.

4. To fill in the time while waiting for the cake to finish baking, make birthday cards to give to the honored child. Decorate the cards with crayons or construction paper scraps.

From *More Paper, Paint, and Stuff*, published by Scott, Foresman and Company. Copyright © 1989 Karen B. Kurtz and Mark A. Kurtz.

Breakfast Celebration

Each Child Needs:

one 9x12-inch sheet of drawing paper

crayons

pencil

The Group Needs:

assorted cooking utensils and equipment

breakfast foods from three countries

small plastic bowls and cups

plastic spoons

newspapers to cover working area

Procedure:

1. Just for fun, create an international breakfast celebration!

2. Choose breakfast foods from three countries. Locate the countries on a map or globe.

3. Prepare the foods. Eat and enjoy!

4. Use crayons to draw a picture about the breakfast experience. Label which of the three foods was the favorite.

From *More Paper, Paint, and Stuff*, published by Scott, Foresman and Company, Copyright © 1989 Karen B. Kurtz and Mark A. Kurtz.

Origami Tulip

Each Child Needs:

one 8x8-inch sheet of red, orange, or pink tissue paper or gift wrap for the tulip

one 9x12-inch sheet of white drawing paper for the background

two 1x6-inch strips of green construction paper for the stem and leaves

scissors

glue

From *More Paper, Paint, and Stuff*, published by Scott, Foresman and Company. Copyright © 1989 Karen B. Kurtz and Mark A. Kurtz.

Procedure:

1. Fold the tissue paper or gift wrap in half diagonally to make a folded triangle shape.

2. Fold in half again, and make a small mark on the center of the fold line. Unfold.

3. Place the folded triangle so that the fold is nearest you.

4. Fold up the right corner of the paper at an angle, using the mark at the center of the fold line as a visual guide.

5. Repeat step 4 for the left side. These two folded corners and the one between them make the tulip's three pointed "petals."

6. To make the tulip's stem, glue a strip of green construction paper to the background sheet.

7. Glue the tulip over the stem.

8. Cut large leaves from the remaining strip of green construction paper, and glue in place.

From *More Paper, Paint, and Stuff,* published by Scott, Foresman and Company. Copyright © 1989 Karen B. Kurtz and Mark A. Kurtz.

Skyscrapers

Each Child Needs:

crayons

The Group Needs:

assorted sheets of construction paper, about 6x18 inches, 6x9 inches, and/or 12x18 inches

Procedure:

1. Talk about skyscrapers.

2. Use crayons to draw a skyscraper on the construction paper. Make the building as big as the sheet of paper.

3. Read and talk further about skyscrapers.

Variations:

1. Assemble all the skyscrapers into a "skyline" display.

2. Cut windows or doors in the skyscrapers.

3. From construction paper scraps, create cut-out people to work inside the skyscrapers. Glue the paper figures behind windows and doors. Add crayon accents.

From *More Paper, Paint, and Stuff*, published by Scott, Foresman and Company. Copyright © 1989 Karen B. Kurtz and Mark A. Kurtz.

A Passover Meal

Advance Adult Preparation:

The Jewish holiday of Passover is celebrated in the spring. Symbolizing the passing over of the Israelites from slavery to freedom, the holiday lasts eight days. Read the story in Exodus 12:3-40 or find other books in the library that describe the special significance of the Passover foods.

Each Child Needs:

a plastic plate

plastic forks and spoons

a napkin

a plastic cup or glass for grape juice

The Group Needs:

lamb

unleavened bread or crackers

hard-boiled eggs

parsley dipped in water

apples

nuts

grape juice

assorted measuring utensils

large bowls for mixing

other preparation supplies as needed

Procedure:

1. Prepare the Passover meal, called a Seder, with these foods: lamb, unleavened bread or crackers, hard-boiled eggs, parsley dipped in water, apples, and nuts. Since there are no specified quantities or methods of preparation, you can creatively adapt the meal to fit your situation.

2. Talk about how these foods relate to the escape of the Jewish people from slavery in Egypt.

3. Eat and enjoy!

Variations:

1. Set a fancy table with a tablecloth and candles. Provide a special environment for this feast.

2. Combine several of the Passover foods—e.g., Waldorf salad from apples and nuts.

3. Visit a Jewish deli and talk about other special foods.

Oriental Lantern

Each Child Needs:

one 1x12-inch strip of black construction paper for the handle

crayons

one 9x12-inch sheet of white drawing paper for the lantern

glue

Procedure:

1. Use crayons to draw small flower or tree motifs on the paper. Press the crayons heavily onto the paper.

2. With the decorated side of the paper facing out, fold the paper in half, matching the long edges.

3. Beginning at the fold line, cut straight lines across the paper in about one-inch strips. Stop each cut about one inch from the edge.

4. Carefully unfold the paper.

5. Roll the paper into a circle and glue at the top and bottom. This makes the oriental lantern. The lantern should remain open in the middle.

6. Glue the handle inside the lantern.

7. Stand the lantern on a table.

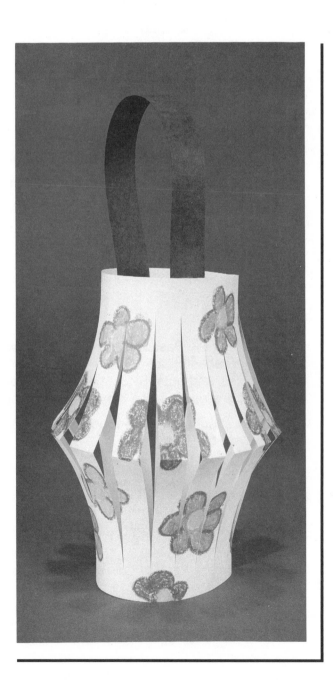

From *More Paper, Paint, and Stuff,* published by Scott, Foresman and Company, Copyright © 1989 Karen B. Kurtz and Mark A. Kurtz.

More Helpful Hints

Blown Eggs: You can empty raw eggs and then decorate the shells. Start by gently piercing a needle into both ends of an egg. Then, holding the egg over a bowl, blow hard into the hole at one end. The contents of the egg will exit through the hole at the other end. After rinsing the egg well with water, you can proceed to decorate the shell.

Collage: A collage is a collection of various objects or materials, either flat or dimensional, glued to a background.

Colored Pasta: Pour rubbing alcohol and food coloring into a small bowl. Fill the bowl with pasta. Then, after making sure that the pasta remains under the liquid, let it stand until the pasta reaches the desired color. Dry and drain the pasta. String or paste the colored pasta into decorations.

Crayon Removal: Turpentine will dissolve crayon, and sandpaper will abrade it away.

Crayon Resist: A crayon resist is based on the fact that crayoned areas resist paint. Start by pressing crayons down heavily on paper while creating a drawing. Then brush a tempera or watercolor paint wash quickly and lightly over the surface of the paper.

Cutting on the Fold: Teach children to hold the folded paper in one hand between thumb and index finger. Then cut along the open edges (in most cases) to prevent cutting the wrong side and to avoid creating two halves instead of one whole object.

Finger Paint: You can make your own finger paints by mixing wallpaper paste into cold or tepid water and stirring until smooth. Add color pigment and pour into containers.

Fixative: To prevent smudging, spray completed pictures with hairspray or a commercial fixative. This technique works well for wet or dry chalk pictures, charcoal drawings, and pencil sketches.

Glue Wash: Use water to thin glue to a desired consistency and then brush on paper. A glue wash comes in handy for tissue paper projects or other see-through activities where glue itself would be too thick.

Mobiles: For an individual mobile, you can use a straight branch, a dowel rod, or a bent wire coat hanger as a base. For a group mobile, try suspending a hula hoop, old bicycle tire, or metal ring from the ceiling. You can balance most mobiles by changing the position of objects on the base.

Paint Containers: Use small aluminum pie pans or square trays, paper milk cartons with their tops removed, or small glass jars with lids as water or paint containers.

Paint Dispensers: Empty and clean plastic squeeze containers from mustard, catsup, or syrup—or squirt-top bottles from dishwashing detergent—make easy-to-use paint dispensers.

Parchment Paper: You can make your own parchment paper by brushing linseed oil on one side of cream-colored or white paper. Then brush the other side with turpentine, and allow the paper to dry.

Picture Framing: Here are some ways to highlight and display special artwork: (1) Cut a piece of white cardboard, mat board, or construction paper larger than the artwork. Allow at least two inches on the top and sides of the picture, and at least two and one-half inches on the bottom. Mount and glue the artwork on top of this background. (2) Spray an old picture frame with gold paint and mat the inner portion with velvet. Mount the artwork inside the frame. (3) Purchase inexpensive plastic frames (available in all sizes, from large poster to small desktop frames) and slip the artwork inside. (4) For especially worthy projects, copy the artwork onto a burlap frame, and then hook yarn pieces into the burlap. You can use this method—an extra special way to preserve artwork permanently—to create a latch-hook rug, chair pad, or pillow. (5) Take the artwork to a commercial framing shop and have it mounted under nonglare glass.

Salt and Cornstarch Play Dough: Cook two cups of salt, one cup of cornstarch, and one and one-half cups of water in a double boiler until it forms a mass. Place the mass on waxed paper. When it is cool enough to handle, add food coloring and knead it for about three minutes. Wrap in foil until time for use. Then knead again right before using. This recipe is especially well suited for projects that involve modeling techniques around wire.

Salt and Flour Play Dough: Measure three cups of flour and mix with one and one-half cups of table salt in a bowl. Add water and a few drops of food coloring until the consistency is like bread dough. Mix thoroughly. If stored in a plastic bag, the dough will keep for about a week.

Salt Beads: Mix two parts table salt and one part flour with enough water to create a dough-like consistency. Add food coloring, if desired. Then form into beads, and use a toothpick to pierce a hole in each bead. Allow the beads to dry before stringing.

Soda and Cornstarch Sculpture: Combine two cups of cornstarch, four cups of baking soda, and two and one-half cups of water in a saucepan. Cook over medium heat, stirring constantly. When the mixture has thickened to a dough-like consistency, turn out onto aluminum foil. Cool slightly before working in food coloring. Roll or cut the clay into small shapes. Store any extra clay in aluminum foil.

From *More Paper, Paint, and Stuff*, published by Scott, Foresman and Company, Copyright © 1989 Karen B. Kurtz and Mark A. Kurtz.

Sponge Painting: Cut one-inch squares from sponges, dip the squares into paint, and then print on paper. You can then wash, dry and reuse the sponge squares.

Stitchery: A variety of sewing stitches can create texture and add interest to stitchery. Use walking stitches (short even stitches on top of and underneath the fabric), running stitches (long stitches on top with short stitches underneath the fabric), and jumping stitches (long angled stitches either close together or far apart on the fabric. You can sew yarn on burlap or mesh produce bags.

Tempera Paint for Glossy Surfaces: By mixing liquid detergent into tempera paint you enable the paint to stick to aluminum foil, glass, or oily surfaces.

Tempera Paint Wash: A tempera paint wash is diluted paint that is brushed quickly and lightly onto the paper. To prepare the wash, add two tablespoons of tempera paint to about a pint of water. Experiment before using in order to adjust the color tint.

Time-Saving Techniques: (1) Capitalize on the fact that children learn from and are stimulated by each other; working in groups benefits the children as it saves time for you. (2) Have groups of children do different activities simultaneously; for example, one group can take turns at the work area while other groups write stories, read books, or listen to tapes. (3) Group together for "messy" activities like painting, cooking, and water projects or when materials are limited. (4) Provide enough newspapers to cover the working area adequately; newspapers can make clean-up time a breeze! (5) Establish separate work areas for each of the various steps of a complicated project; for example, have the children select colored fabric in one area, draw a picture of a clown in another area, and stack their finished projects in yet another area.

Title: Encourage children to title some of their artwork. Doing so enhances both personal expression and creativity and may even improve language arts skills.

Watercolor Painting: Use two jars of water with watercolor activities. One jar is for washing the brushes to keep them "pure." The second jar is then used for picking up clean water to add to the concentrated watercolor.

Wet Chalk: To intensify colors and create a fixative, briefly dip construction paper in water before applying colored chalk.

Red-Tongued Monster

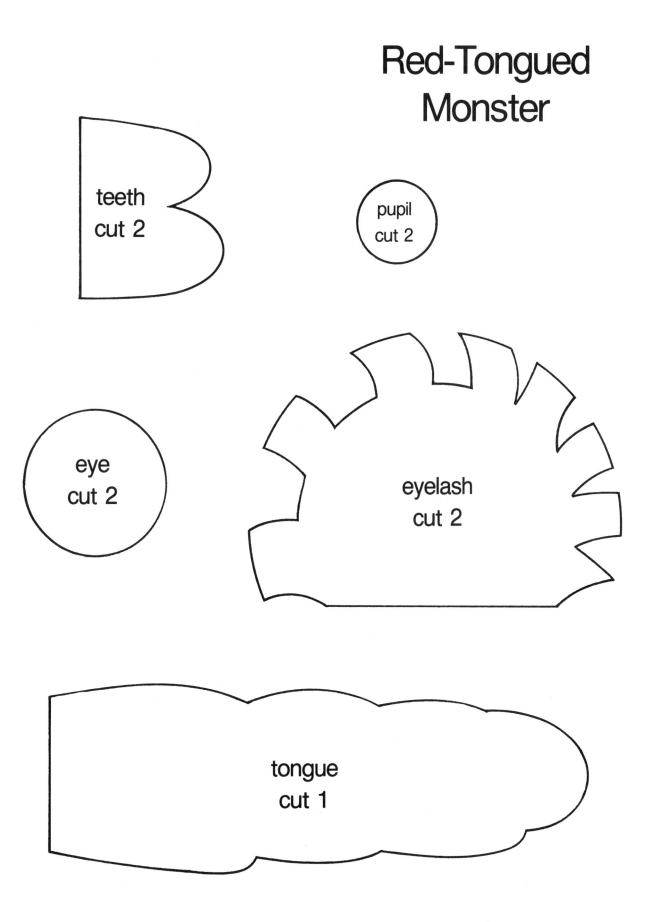

teeth
cut 2

pupil
cut 2

eye
cut 2

eyelash
cut 2

tongue
cut 1

House

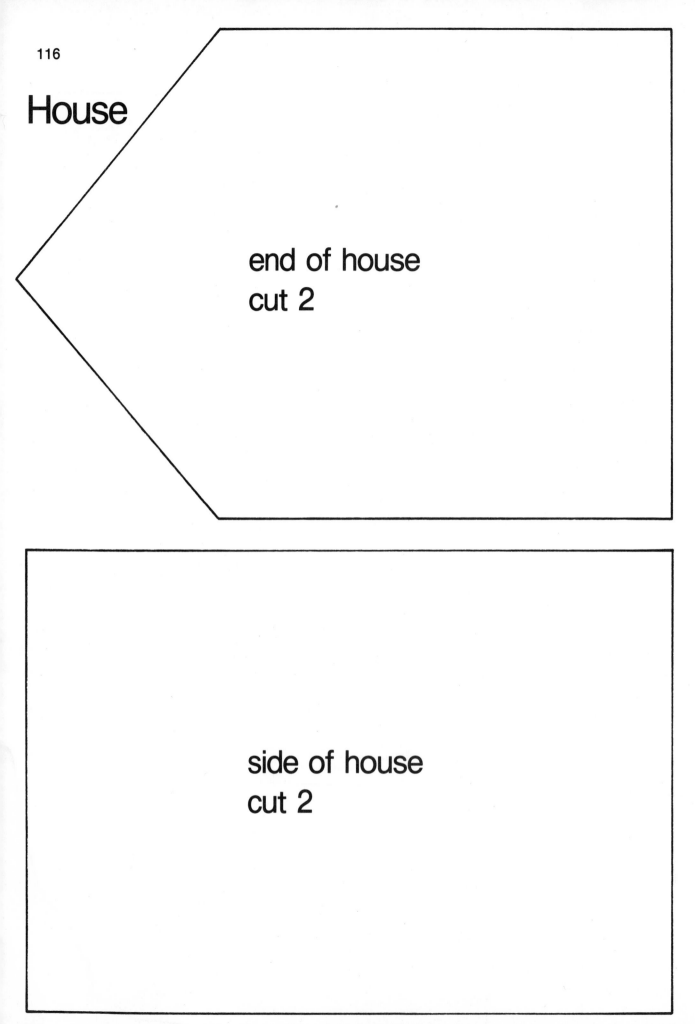

end of house
cut 2

side of house
cut 2

From *More Paper, Paint, and Stuff*, published by Scott, Foresman and Company. Copyright © 1989 Karen B. Kurtz and Mark A. Kurtz.

Boo!

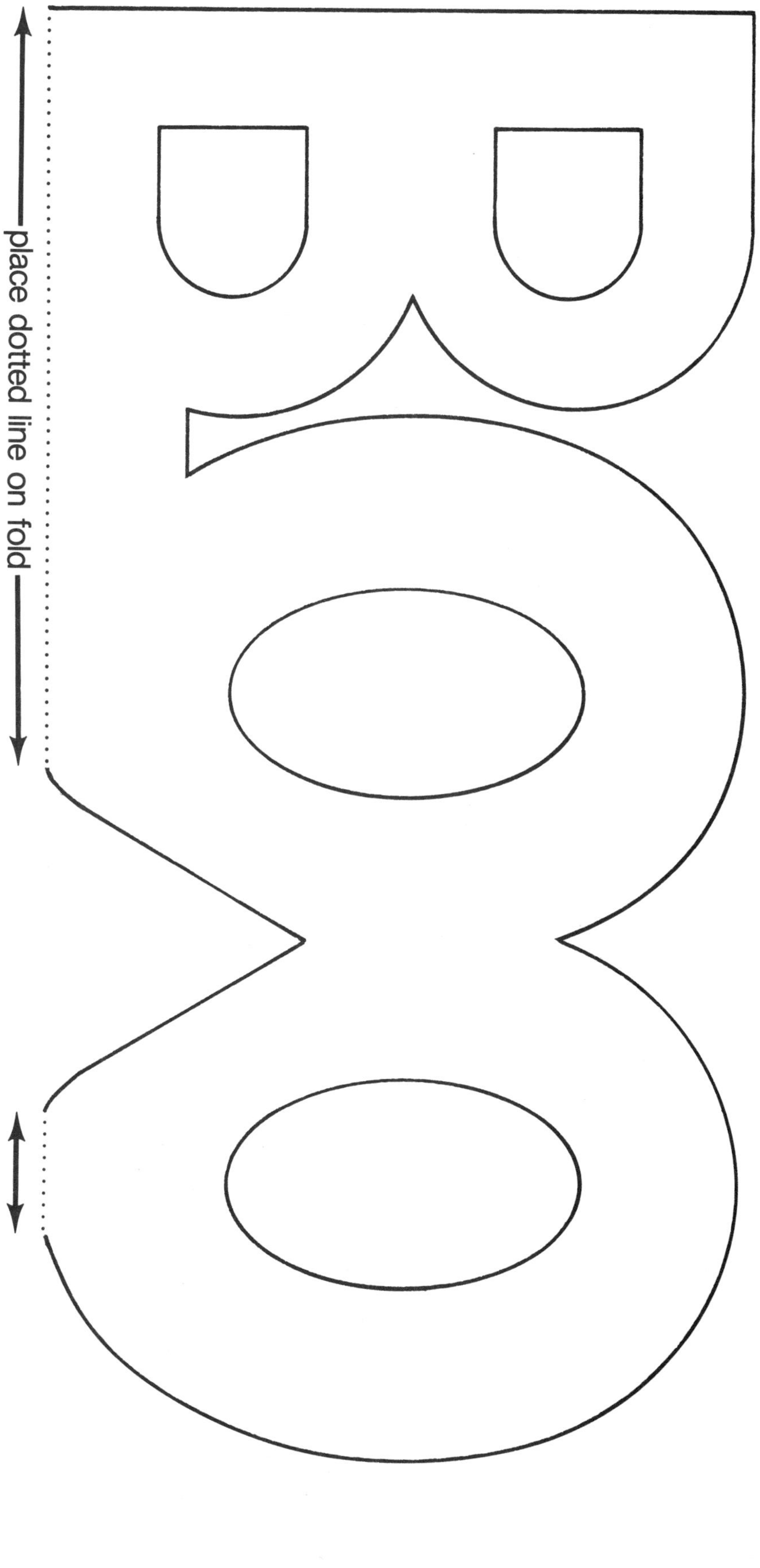

place dotted line on fold

Indian Mask

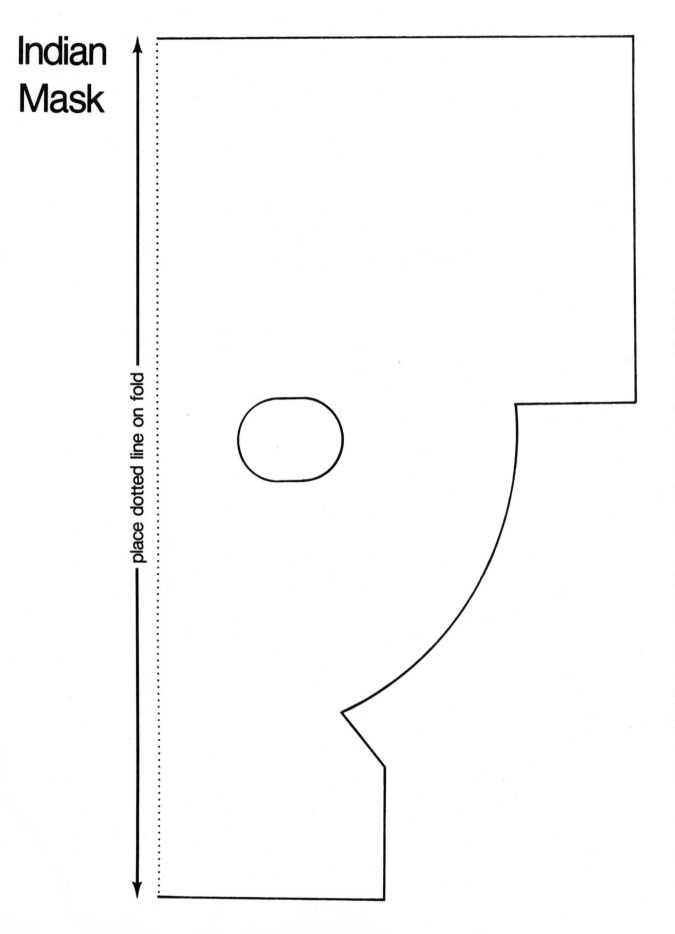

place dotted line on fold

Turkey Mask

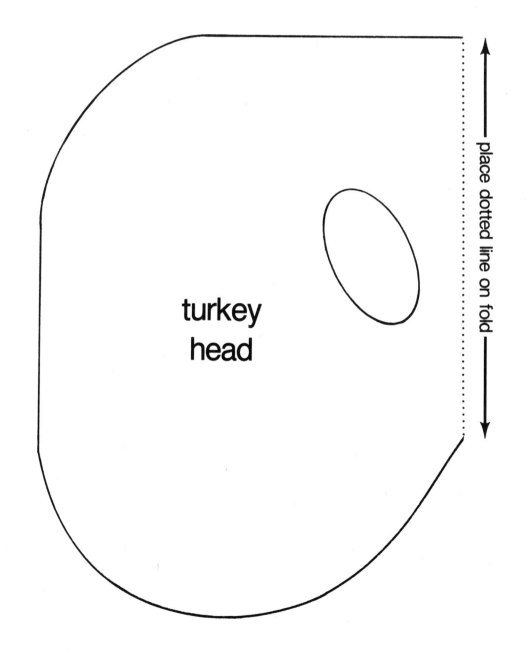

turkey
head

place dotted line on fold

Birthday Crown

place dotted line on fold

cut 2

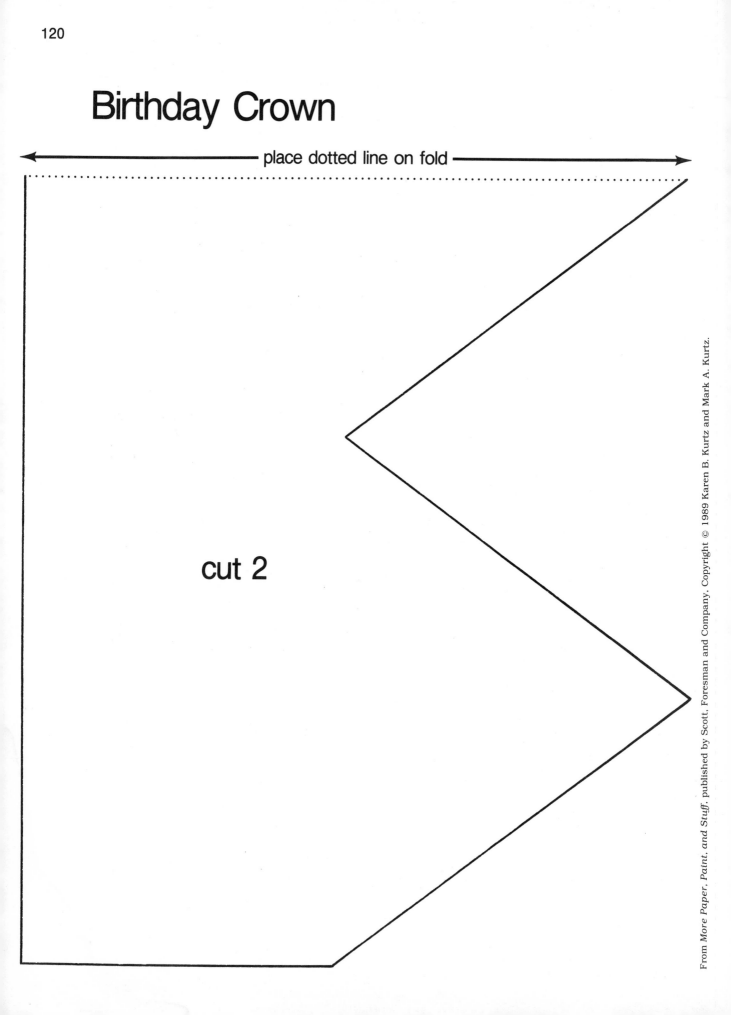

From *More Paper, Paint, and Stuff,* published by Scott, Foresman and Company. Copyright © 1989 Karen B. Kurtz and Mark A. Kurtz.

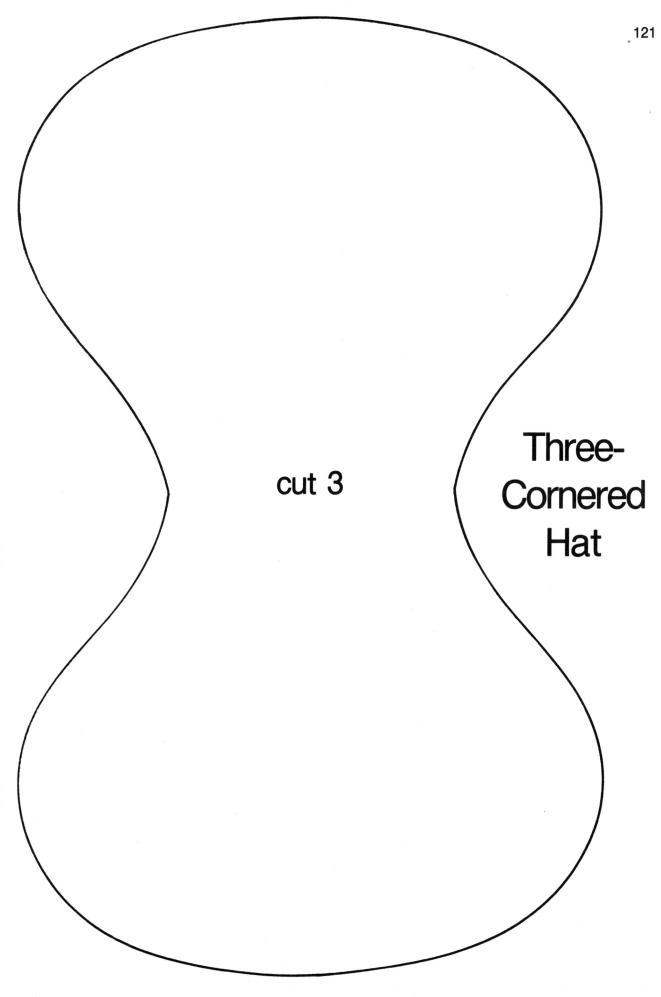

cut 3

Three-Cornered Hat

Open Windows

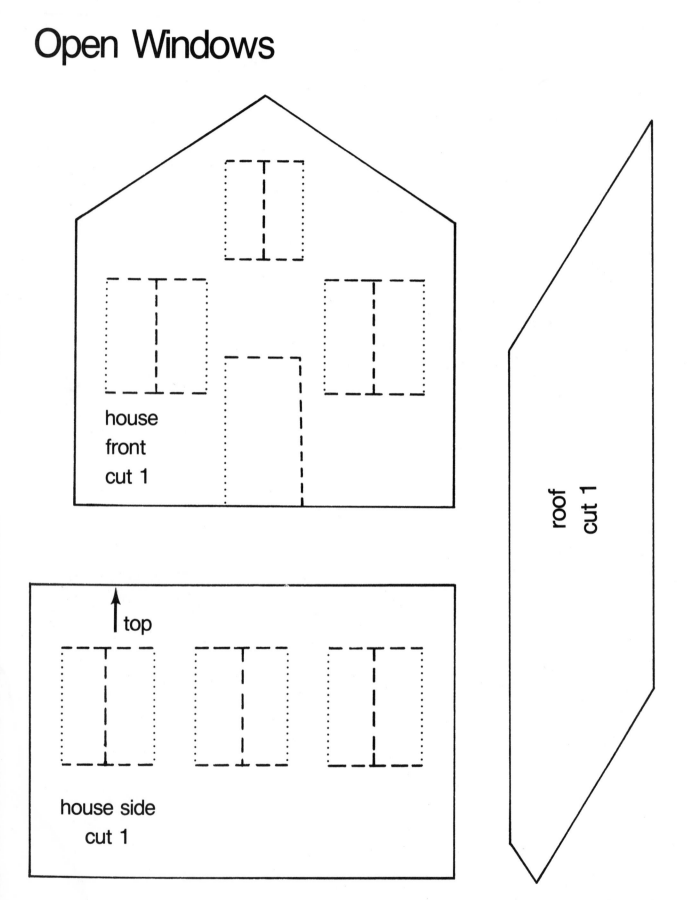

house
front
cut 1

top

house side
cut 1

roof
cut 1

From *More Paper, Paint, and Stuff*, published by Scott, Foresman and Company. Copyright © 1989 Karen B. Kurtz and Mark A. Kurtz.

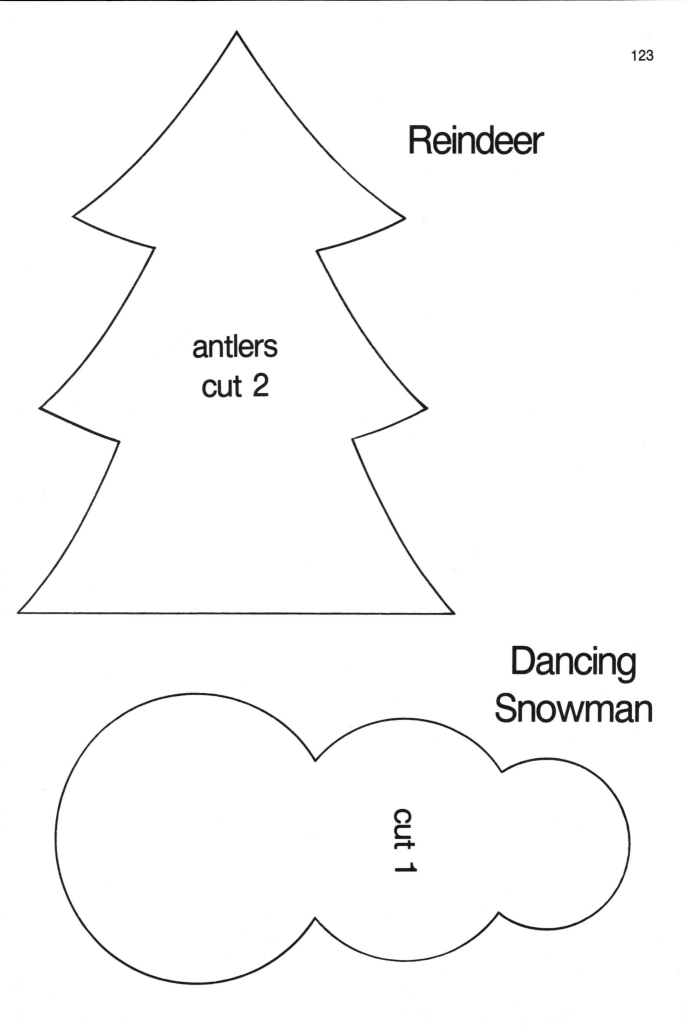

Reindeer

antlers
cut 2

Dancing
Snowman

cut 1

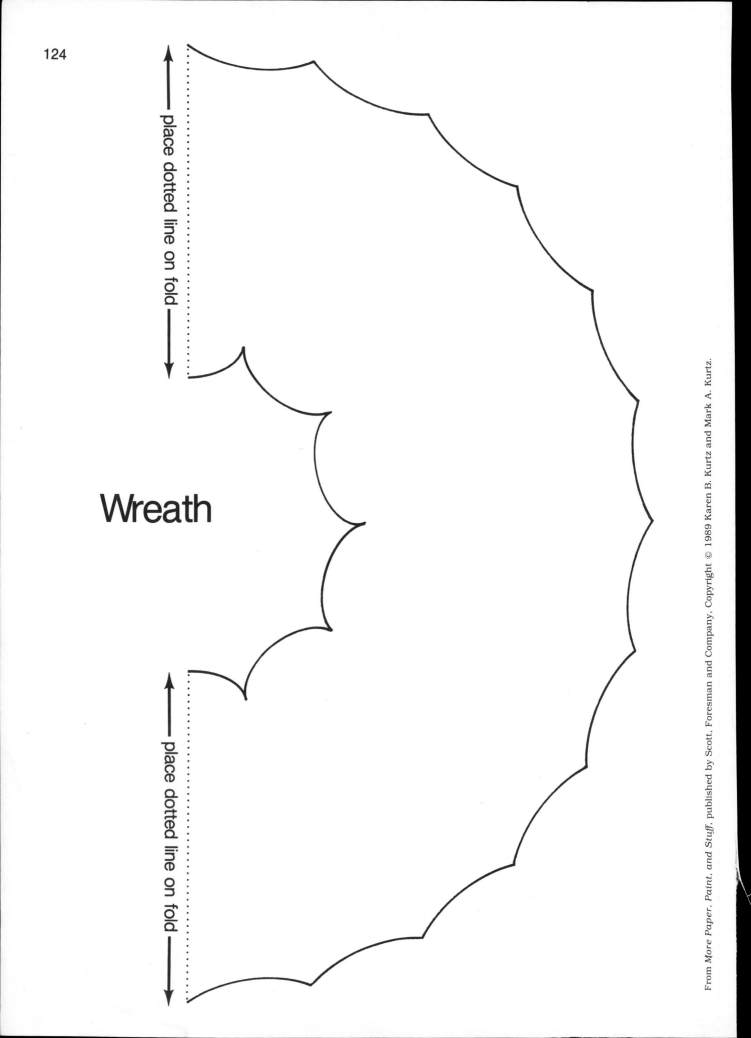

124

place dotted line on fold

Wreath

place dotted line on fold

From *More Paper, Paint, and Stuff*, published by Scott, Foresman and Company. Copyright © 1989 Karen B. Kurtz and Mark A. Kurtz.

Butterfly

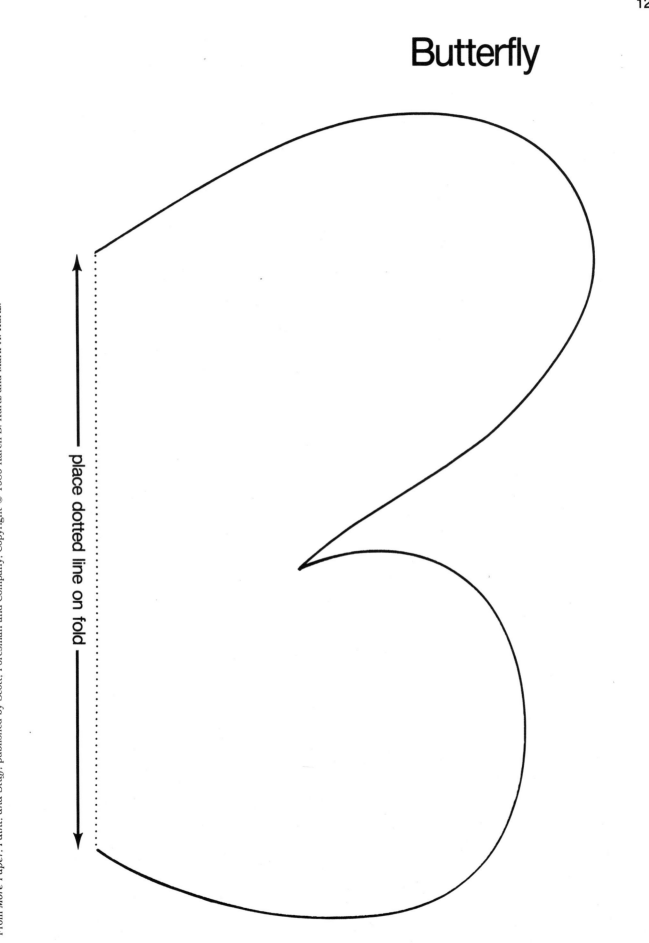

place dotted line on fold

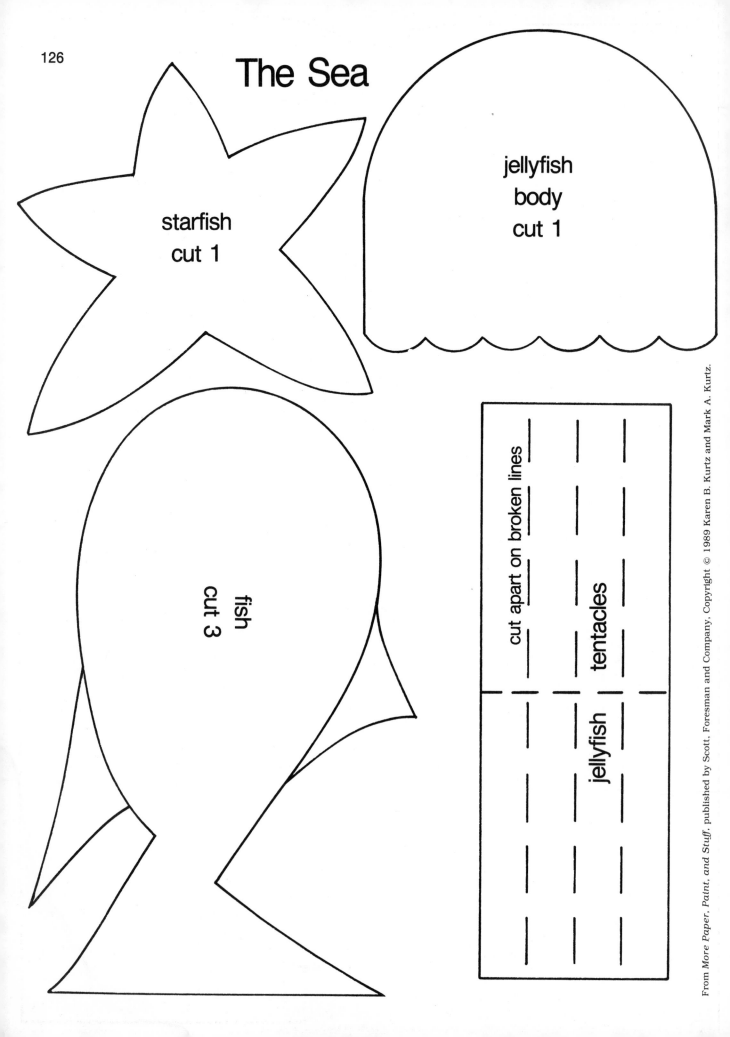

The Sea

starfish
cut 1

jellyfish
body
cut 1

fish
cut 3

cut apart on broken lines

tentacles

jellyfish

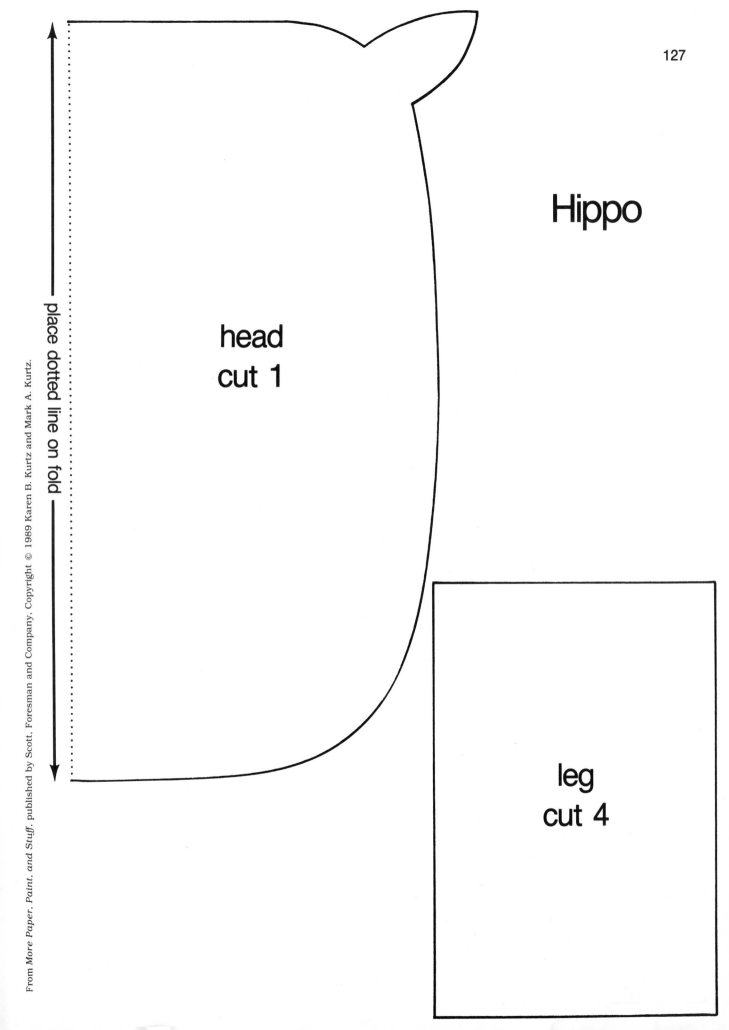

127

Hippo

head
cut 1

place dotted line on fold

leg
cut 4

Hippo (continued)

◄─────── place dotted line on fold ───────►

cut
apart
on
broken
lines

From *More Paper, Paint, and Stuff*, published by Scott, Foresman and Company. Copyright © 1989 Karen B. Kurtz and Mark A. Kurtz.

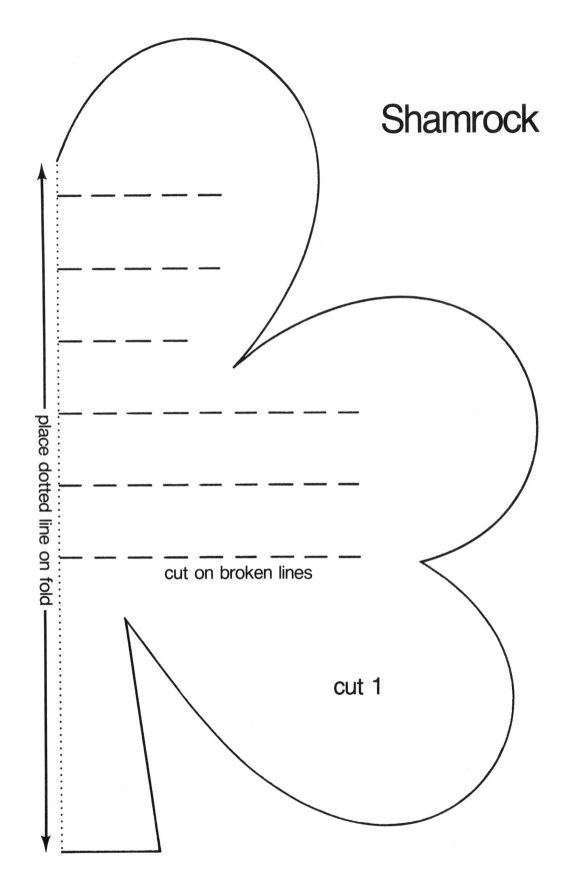

Shamrock

place dotted line on fold

cut on broken lines

cut 1

Valentine Packet

cut 1

Tannenbaum

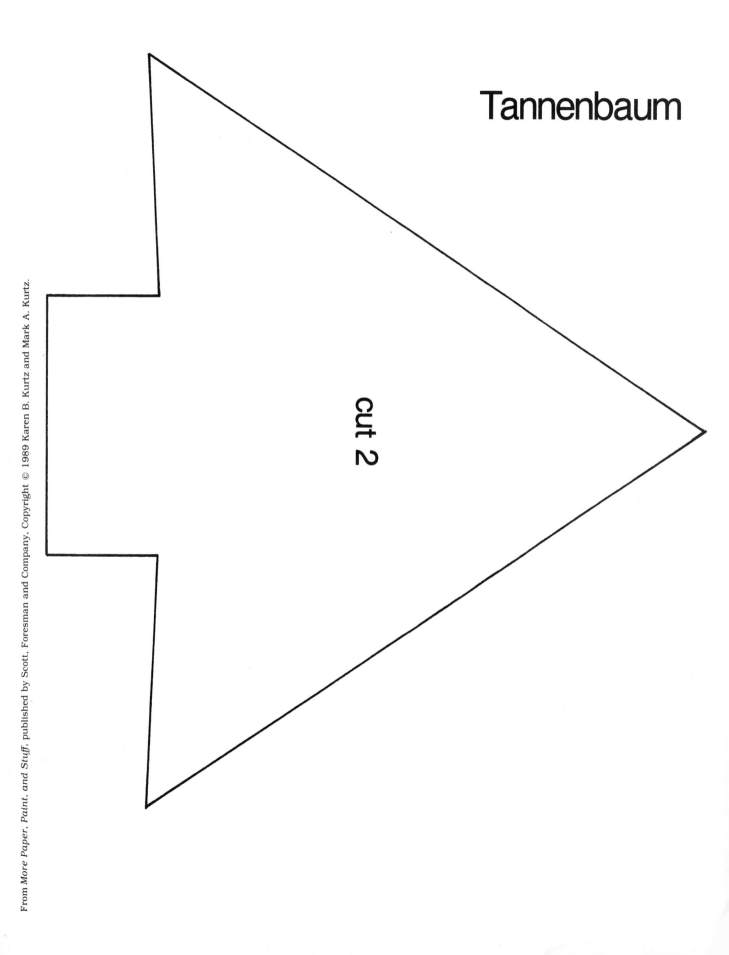

cut 2

Star Magnet
and
Tin Punch Star

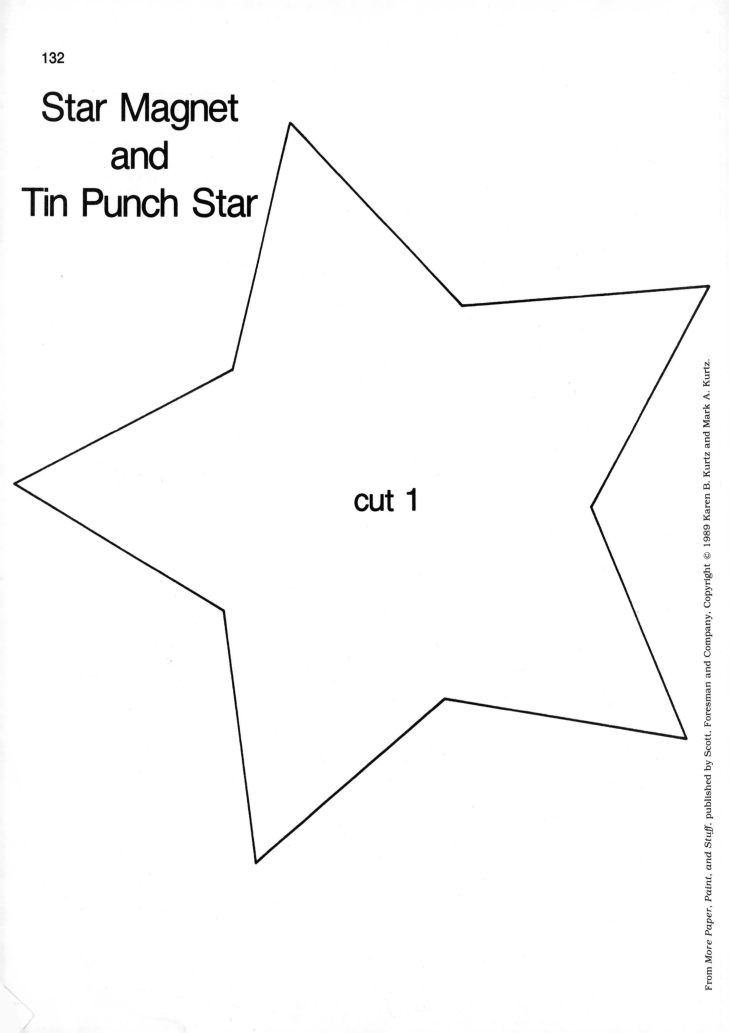

cut 1

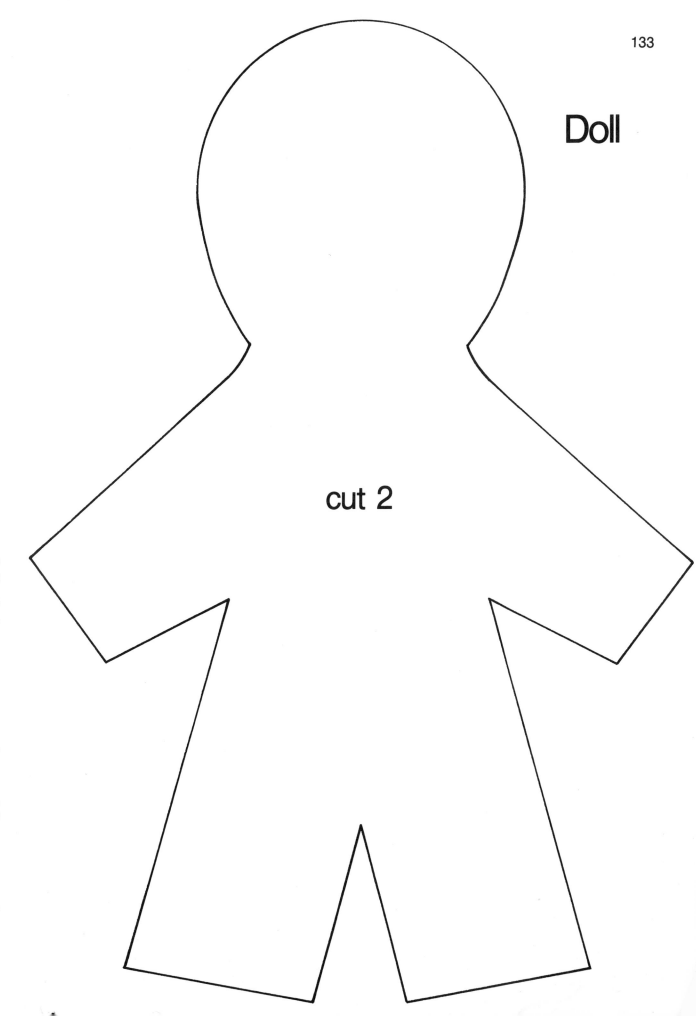

Doll

cut 2